12 Virtues of a Good Teacher

BR. LUKE M. GRANDE, F.S.C.

12
VIRTUES
~C~ OF A ~S~
GOOD
TEACHER

SOPHIA INSTITUTE PRESS
Manchester, New Hampshire

Nihil obstat: John R. Ready, *Censor Librorum*
March 20, 1962
Imprimatur: ✠ Robert F. Joyce, Bishop of Burlington
March 21, 1962
Cum Permissu Superiorum: Br. Charles Henry, F.S.C.,
Assistant Superior General for the United States and Missions
Rome, Italy, January 27, 1962

Sophia Institute Press
Box 5284, Manchester, NH 03108
1-800-888-9344

www.SophiaInstitute.com

Sophia Institute Press® is a registered trademark of Sophia Institute.

paperback ISBN 978-1-64413-812-0

ebook ISBN 978-1-64413-813-7

Library of Congress Control Number: 2022948650

First printing

To

St. Jean-Baptiste de La Salle
Patron of All Teachers

In packs they prowled the city street by night;
through silence shouted anguished cries by day;
rebellion surged about their brash dismay
at worlds in which they feared they had no right.
Where was apocalyptic word, the blight
to heal? Where hand, the timeless crooked way
to clear? Where heart, the cheerless chamber's gray
to feel? Would no one give them back their sight?
God sent to them a man disarmed by love
and "Suffer little children," His own word,
to wash away their cares and turn above
a voiceless prayer the world had never heard.
His road through Rheims could only be a part
of this, His answer: word and hand and heart.

— *Youth*, May 1962

Contents

Note on the 2022 Printing

This book is outdated—not for what it says but for what it doesn't say.

Absent is any discussion of how virtue will help us to train our students in the most efficient standardized-test-taking strategies or to incorporate the latest technology into our lessons every day. You won't find references to how virtue will improve benchmarks, standards, or curriculum frameworks, help us conduct "virtual classes," or even provide "social-emotional learning" experiences.

It is in this apparent lack of relevance to today's challenges that *12 Virtues of a Good Teacher* is the most relevant book for Catholic educators in any setting today: from homeschooling parents to Catholic school teachers to those teaching in public schools. It is a book on teaching from the time before progressive reformers tried to make teaching into a science, or more properly, a *technique*, the time before practitioners were required to be licensed by the state and teaching became full of processes and procedures, standardized units of advancement, and so-called measurable outcomes, rather than being acknowledged as a thoroughly human, incarnational endeavor.

Like the virtues, so many of the struggles and joys teachers experience are universal. For example, haven't we all, old and new teachers alike, been tempted to let classroom discipline slide because we want to be well liked, as the author describes in his chapter on wisdom? And don't all of us teachers, joyfully passionate as we are about our subject matter, need prudence to remember that we teach not our subject but young human beings?

And every teacher always needs the correct understanding of piety—a virtue that has fallen out of favor these days. Through the virtue of piety, the good teacher

> in a thousand ways reveals to his students every day the depth and reality of his devotion to God.... In being a practical, living example of Christian piety, the teacher as teacher best gives God His due and provides students with an ideal of piety to emulate. But, anomalously, *when the teacher turns his eyes away from God and looks at himself to see whether or not he is being an example to the students, his piety becomes calculation and he fails on both counts—as dutiful creature and living example. The teacher's religious "edification" of students must be the overflow from his own genuine religious activity.*... We will make a greater impression on them by a wise and modest conduct than by a multitude of words. (emphasis added)

As we read in this discussion on what it means to witness to the Christian life—and throughout every chapter—we must admit that 12 Virtues of a Good Teacher is also "outdated" in its correct understanding of means and ends, unlike much of modern education, which tends to confuse the two.

With the proper understanding of the virtues of good teachers, we see that working out our own salvation is the best way to help our students become the saints God calls them to be. So whether you're just starting out or are a veteran of the classroom, whether you teach your own children or a classroom of thirty teenagers, may you find in these pages a vision of education that helps you on this journey.

Foreword

The effectiveness of teachers is largely dependent on their contact with a tradition of active teaching. For teaching is of its nature a continuous process. Teaching conveys the experience of the past through the present to the future. The fact that a good teacher inevitably fecundates his material in a special vision of his own does not mean that the life he gives it is utterly new. Like other life on this earth, it is continuous in some way with what went before. Its very freshness and newness and unexpectedness attest its contact with that part of the teaching tradition that is alive. Even the successful educational reformer is not one who has had no contact with other teachers but one who has learned more from them, directly or indirectly, than most men do.

St. Jean-Baptiste de La Salle was an educational reformer whose particular vision should commend itself to the modern world, since he wanted Christian education to extend not merely to those interested in classical studies but to other groups in society as well. Nevertheless, despite his revolutionary ambitions, he was, as every good revolutionary is, within a live teaching tradition. Br. Luke M. Grande, F.S.C., has here dipped back into that tradition, seizing on the twelve virtues that St. La Salle thought necessary for a good teacher and using them as foci for his own discussion of some of the requisites for a Christian teacher today.

With full historical awareness and pointed documentation, he makes it clear that no great theological or philosophical issues hinge upon this particular selection or enumeration of virtues. Generally speaking, he uses the English names for them—such as seriousness, silence, humility, wisdom, patience—with the range of meanings that such terms commonly have in English, controlling the range in whatever way his discussion demands. This is a well-warranted procedure for the present purposes because it enables Br. Luke to structure his discussion within a framework that is adaptable to the present without being out of touch with the past.

The considerations that he proposes are not formally philosophical or coldly methodological but meditative—and in a practical way. We overhear in these pages the unidentified voices of living or once-living men with whom the author is in living contact and to whose voices and convictions he adds his own. We catch particularly the voices of the Brothers of the Christian Schools, who, from the seventeenth century to the twentieth, have been teaching thoughtfully, alertly, and reflectively, trying always to keep their performance in line with the needs of humanity and with Christian ideals. From the seventeenth century to the twentieth, curricula have changed, but concern for the integrity of subject matter, whatever it is, and for those who come to the teacher to learn are abiding preoccupations that register strongly here.

This is not a book about teachers except insofar as it is a book for teachers. It is for those who are actually teaching, those who have taught and still like to think about it, or those who ambition teaching. It treats its subject inspirationally—and understandably so. No one burns more with enthusiasm for his work than a good teacher, sensing as he does that his work of teaching is the summary activity of mankind, dealing with the core of human experience, communicating from person to person what has been distilled out of this experience since man's first appearance on our globe. To the enthusiasm that this sense fosters, the Christian adds more, since he sees teaching as reflecting, however slightly, the work of Jesus Christ, the Word of God, Himself God, communicated and communicating to man. As the growing complexity of civilization makes life more and more dependent on teaching, the enthusiasm as well as the meditative reflection we find here should stand us in good stead.

—Walter J. Ong, S.J.
Saint Louis University

Preface

12 Virtues of a Good Teacher is written for all Christian teachers working in all types of schools: public or private, nonsectarian or denominational.

It is not essentially a philosophical or theological dissertation nor a book about methodology; rather, it presents in untechnical language a conception of the ideal teacher.

The virtues of the good teacher are considered here in a practical, social context: not "humility" but "humility for a teacher"; not "wisdom" but the "wisdom of a teacher" — for it is in his vocation as a teacher that he will perfect himself as a Christian.

Since it is by being "good" that, to a great extent, he will teach "well," the ambivalence of the word *good* in the title is intentional.

No doubt the beginning teacher should find this work most useful, but it may recall to the experienced teacher, as well, many old truths. The ideas are as ancient as Christianity and are offered without claim to being revolutionary, except in the sense that the ideal presented by Christ was indeed revolutionary.

To a teacher trained in Catholic universities, it might be slightly "old hat"; nevertheless, in looking at these reflections closely and afresh, he may also find some use in them.

To anyone involved in this massive project, modern education, it is hoped that the book may prove helpful.

History of the Text

"Each generation must write its own books," someone has said. Perhaps "rewrite" would have been a more accurate word. Whatever the truth of the statement, it certainly holds good for *12 Virtues of a Good Teacher*, which goes back initially to the second decade of the eighteenth century.[1]

When St. Jean-Baptiste de La Salle (1651–1719), patron of all teachers, established his congregation, the Brothers of the Christian Schools, in France in the seventeenth century, he found nothing of really practical use with which to form his young and inexperienced teachers. To fill the gap, he himself wrote a book entitled *Conduct of the Christian Schools*, a landmark in works of modern pedagogy: detailed and sensible, it spelled out virtually every move a novice teacher must make in the classroom and out of it.

Of special interest, however, was a simple list, at the end of the *Conduct*, of twelve virtues necessary for a "good master": seriousness, silence, humility, prudence, wisdom, patience, restraint, gentleness, zeal, watchfulness, piety, and generosity.

But the list was not elaborated on until Br. Agathon, superior general of the Christian Brothers, wrote in 1785 an explanation of each virtue. These explanations were published separately as *The Twelve Virtues of a Good Master*. Br. Agathon retained the original listing of virtues, except to substitute *gravity* for *seriousness*, *discretion*

---

[1]   Br. Henri, secretary of the Institute Archives in Rome, has published a fuller account of early editions of the *Twelve Virtues*: "Les douze vertus d'un bon Maître, édition princeps et réédition," Bulletin des Frères des Écoles Chrétiennes 42 (July 1961): 86–90.

for *restraint*, *meekness* and *firmness* for *gentleness*, and *vigilance* for *watchfulness*. The virtues were defined, with their special traits and those opposed to them, and fortified with scriptural passages. The treatise was masterfully written, with clarity, precision, and an eye to the practical.

Later it was bound with the *Management of the Christian Schools* (1887), which was a new edition of the original *Conduct of the Christian Schools*. Several completely new chapters, dealing with subjects not covered in the *Conduct*, were added in the *Management*, and the whole work was adapted to changing needs.

With time came the inevitable need for revision of the *Twelve Virtues* in style and content, to give the work greater immediacy. Br. Agathon's revised list of St. La Salle's original choice of twelve virtues was in turn expanded, this time to twenty-two virtues. Not published as a separate entity, the essays on these twenty-two virtues became integral chapters in the 1922 edition of *Considerations for Christian Teachers*.

The *Considerations* consisted of seventy-two meditations, which, although written as an independent work rather than as a revision of the *Twelve Virtues* and widened, as to scope of subjects discussed, well beyond the simple virtues of a good teacher, followed to some extent Br. Agathon's format (definition, traits, opposing traits).

In addition to the Scriptures, which had been used by Br. Agathon, the works of Fénelon, Bossuet, Gerson, Verniolles, Chrysostom, and, especially, St. La Salle, were heavily drawn upon for the developing of the meditation subjects.

The whole work, *Considerations for Christian Teachers*, was published under the aegis of Br. Philip, assistant to the superior general of the Brothers.

In 1959, the *Considerations* was abridged and revised by a number of teachers under the supervision and coordination of

Br. Francis Patrick. This edition is virtually unchanged from the original *Considerations* of 1922, except for occasional words: substitutions for archaic forms or dated diction.

The resulting work was published and well received under the title *As Stars for All Eternity: Meditations for Teachers*.

The London District of the Brothers of the Christian Schools did very much the same thing in 1960; but instead of using Br. Philip's *Considerations*, as Br. Francis Patrick had done, they returned for their editing and emendation to the text of Br. Agathon's original *Twelve Virtues of a Good Master*.

New Version of the Twelve Virtues

The inception of the present explanation of the *Twelve Virtues* dates back to 1956, when the Christian Brothers Educational Association (CBEA), a national organization composed of Christian Brothers representing all of the districts in the United States, was reorganized into standing committees to work out a complete revision of the 1887 *Management*.

Each district undertook the chairmanship of some particular phase of the *Management* and was to rewrite it in accordance with contemporary needs. This new *Management*, under the general chairmanship of Br. U. Alfred, was to be more than a revised edition; it was to be completely new yet true to the spirit of the original.

Since the *Management* and the *Twelve Virtues*, bound together for convenience in 1887, had been distinct works, the *Twelve Virtues* did not, strictly speaking, come under the heading of "rewriting the *Management*"; however, a fresh explanation of the *Twelve Virtues* was assigned as a special project to the St. Louis District Committee: Brs. Leander Paul (chairman), Louis de La Salle, Kevin Stanislaus, Herbert Lewis, and Maurice.

Their enumeration of the virtues, with a few variations, went back to St. La Salle's simple list as it had appeared in the original *Conduct*. *Seriousness, silence, humility, prudence, wisdom, patience, zeal, piety,* and *generosity* were the same on both St. La Salle's list and the new committee's list; *justice, kindness,* and *firmness* were introduced; and *restraint, gentleness,* and *watchfulness* (treated under *prudence*) were removed.

Once the committee had determined which virtues were to be treated, they epitomized each in a paragraph, deciding definitions and limits.

The work of the committee was then turned over to one writer to elaborate, according to his own views and initiative.

Rewriting the Explanations of the Virtues

When work on the analysis of the virtues began, several changes were ventured.

First of all, the definite article was dropped from the original title; a small point, but one that obviates arguments as to why there are *twelve* (rather than eleven or thirteen) or why the word *the* is used before *virtues*, as though the choice were definitive.

Twelve is not a magic number, but in deference to the traditional twelve of St. La Salle and because such a number allows enough variations in viewpoints from which, flexibly, to study the ideal teacher, twelve was the number decided upon.

Secondly, except for scriptural quotations[2] and incidental references (naturally, St. La Salle's *Meditations* provide a number) that

---

[2] All quotations are taken from the New American Catholic Edition of the Holy Bible with the Confraternity of Christian Doctrine translation of the New Testament and the books of Genesis to Ruth and the books of Job to Sirach (Ecclesiasticus); the remaining books of the Old Testament are the Douay Version. Editor's

entered into the writing, few "authorities" are quoted—a stylistic concession to the tastes of most modern readers for whom such quoting might appear uncongenially pedantic or unnecessary.

Modern methodology resulting from twentieth-century trends or new thinking is implicit throughout, although principles that are perennial and permanent provide, it is hoped, a basic structure for current practice and attitudes.

I wish to thank the members of the national and the local Christian Brothers Educational Association (CBEA) and, especially, Br. U. Alfred, general chairman of the CBEA, for their valuable help and suggestions.

Inadequacies as to content or style are, however, the responsibility of the writer, who was generously given carte blanche in carrying on the work so ably begun by the CBEA Committee for the St. Louis District.

—Br. Luke M. Grande, F.S.C.
Christian Brothers College
Memphis, Tennessee
August 1961

note: All emphases added. Where applicable, the differing names and numbering in the RSV are provided in brackets.

Wisdom

Wise according to God

Where should one begin in discussing the virtues necessary for a good Christian teacher? With kindness? With justice?

Perhaps the best place to start is with wisdom, with which also dwell, according to the Scriptures, counsel, advice, strength, and understanding (Prov. 8:14).

It is not caprice alone or random choice that assigns a preeminent place to wisdom in the hierarchy of necessary virtues for a teacher; for, like a pied piper with everyone trooping at his heels, wisdom is trailed by all of the other virtues.

As the color white contains all the color values of the spectrum, so wisdom contains all the virtues that a good teacher needs. Of wisdom, the Old Testament says: "All good things together came to me in her company, and countless riches at her hands; and I rejoiced in them all, because Wisdom is their leader" (Wisd. 7:11–12).

With such a promise of acquiring all the virtues with one, the teacher does well to ask of God, with the shrewdness of Solomon, "Give me wisdom and knowledge" (2 Par. [Chron.] 1:10), hoping that God will also give him, as He did to Solomon, "wisdom and understanding exceeding much, and largeness of heart as the sand that is on the shore" (3 [1] Kings 4:29).

Wisdom is, therefore, the vade mecum of the teacher, the handbook in which he finds all his answers. When we examine the nature of this virtue, it is easy to see why.

Wisdom sees the integrity of the Divine Plan; by its light, the truly wise man sees — at least in broad outline — the relationship of one truth to another, the beginning and the end of creation, one principle to another.

In a sense, he sees with the eyes of God. With a new kind of knowledge, distinct from that springing merely from college textbooks or laboratories or lectures, the teacher upon whom God has conferred this gift beholds God in everything, recognizes His goodness, and, almost by a kind of intuition, perceives His intentions for all men and all things.

From this lofty eminence, he gains a perspective that sets forth God's picture whole, and each part in its proper place. With the vision attained through wisdom, the teacher can see how he himself fits into God's plan, how his students fit into it as well, and how the whole complex of education helps to accomplish God's design.

To the teacher, confronted with the ancient injunction "Know thyself," comprehensive answers, never dreamed of by the Greek philosophers, are supplied through the wisdom of Christian revelation; and the role of teacher takes on a significance unsuspected by a Socrates.

With new understanding of what man is and his place in the universe, the Christian teacher is better able to comprehend what he should be, what teaching should be, and what its objectives are when he works with God in seeking the total actualization of a student's potentialities for time and for eternity.

Above all, wisdom enables a teacher to discern the part played by his own efforts in the scheme of Divine Providence, his high calling as a cooperator with God in His plans for men.

When he attains this insight into the purposes of Christian education, he sees, further, many of the hazards strewn in his path, ready to cripple him in God's work; and he sees as well many opportunities for good that he might never have been aware of without this vision.

Wisdom, in short, throws a new light on virtually every human activity and relationship; it is, in fact, closely related to the Spirit of Faith (of which St. La Salle speaks in his meditations), which looks upon all things with the eyes of God and attributes all to God.

Effects of Wisdom

The effects of wisdom, moreover, are not merely visionary or theoretical; they are of vital, practical, and far-reaching consequence in actual teaching. For example, a teacher, inflated by his own ego, may begin to neglect class discipline in a misguided attempt to be popular with students; or he may do away with necessary and useful assignments in his subject in order to win over others; or he may compromise his authority and the good he can do in order to be a "pal" to students.

Such tactics can be disastrous and may result from his failure to realize that he has made *himself* the object of his teaching, daily offering up incense to his own image. He has forgotten that he is an instrument to draw out and develop the best in the *students*; that he should be doing God's work, not his own.

On the other hand, if he tries to develop an attractive personality in order to be more effective in doing God's work, he must realize that his effort is furthering the true purposes of education and is not only legitimate but also wise.

Everything will depend on the motive, the angle of vision: the one attitude has distorted the picture; the other has retained the plan.

Students are the first to ferret out the underlying, true motives; they are rarely fooled; they distinguish the popularity seeker from the wise teacher.

Not only himself as teacher but maverick theories of education, weighed in the scales of wisdom, are likewise properly evaluated by the wise teacher.

Much modern educational procedure, for example, is unfortunately posited on the malignant thesis that man is merely a more or less complicated animal (or, at least, spiritual realities are so *ignored* that the results are the same as if they were denied outright).

The teacher committed to such a naturalistic belief trains his students to adjust psychologically or socially to their environment. Since their goal in life is conceived to be perfect happiness on earth, they must be instructed in how to get the most pleasure out of life, how to make the most money, how to make others contribute to their own ease and welfare.

The merely humanitarian principle that is supposed to supply the basis for "good citizenship" or "togetherness" in such an educational philosophy is too tenuous to be really effective. As a consequence, a pragmatic system of values is inculcated in the students. The results are, too frequently, juvenile delinquents (puzzling to their confused teacher and parents) who turn into Machiavellian adults.

What happens when, through the enlightenment of wisdom, the concept of man's immortal soul and the role of the temporal in relation to the eternal are injected into such a system?

Like a jigsaw puzzle, the pieces fit together with new meaning and coherence. While the valid contributions of psychology and modern pedagogy are retained, the actuality of Original Sin, grace, and immortality rearrange educational goals in a newly realistic order.

Learning

Recognizing the necessity for wisdom does not mean that the Christian teacher should embrace a philosophy of ignorance that would leave everything up to God and nothing up to the teacher; knowledge provides a necessary climate for wisdom. "I, Wisdom, dwell with experience, and judicious knowledge I attain," say the Scriptures (Prov. 8:12).

Because wisdom is a virtue, it does not follow that learning is a vice. On the contrary, wisdom itself would dictate the necessity of a teacher's being as completely trained as possible. "It would be a shame if you did not know sufficiently what you have to teach," St. La Salle says in his meditations. "This would be criminal ignorance which would cause the ignorance of your students" (Meditations for Rogation Monday and August 7).

If the teacher's function is to communicate the truth, he must know the truth. Only through constant application to the development of the mind that God has given him will he attain it.

Wisdom will not miraculously provide a teacher with information about the second law of thermodynamics, a valid interpretation of *Hamlet*, or an historically accurate account of the American Civil War (although even here, in a certain manner, it may help). "The mind of the intelligent man seeks knowledge," says Proverbs (15:14), and "The lips of the wise disseminate knowledge" (Prov. 15:7).

What distinguishes the wise teacher from the foolish one is not his ignorance of facts (and reliance on some kind of infused knowledge that burgeons forth without effort) but his ability to put a proper value on them and to place them at the service of the developing student. For a teacher to lack the necessary competence in his subject is to violate a first principle of wisdom.

For example, for him to pronounce pious platitudes in a religion class while failing to acquaint his students with teachings on dogma, morality, and worship—or worse, to purvey false, garbled versions of such doctrines—is to perpetrate a type of scandal "of the little ones," the worst conceivable for a teacher of youth and a kind that Christ severely condemns.

It is not learning but the misuse of learning that is culpable. *The Imitation of Christ* (which is so often and so erroneously charged with anti-intellectualism) maintains that "Learning is not to be blamed, nor the mere knowledge of anything which is good in itself and ordained by God" (I:3:4).

"Worldly Wisdom" versus Wisdom

What is blameworthy is the distortion of learning, that "wisdom of this world" that God has "turned to foolishness" (1 Cor. 1:20). It is the "learned," meaning the intellectually proud, who "are desirous to appear and to be called wise" (*Imitation*, 1:2:2) but whom the Lord knows to be "empty" (1 Cor. 3:19).

Those who are truly wise desire *to be*, not *to seem*, learned, since it is by their learning that they are better able to do God's work; they are interested neither in the world's applause nor in their own self-approbation.

The truly wise man is simple; this is not to say that he is simple-minded. *Simplicity* means "unity, oneness"—the ability to look at all things through the one, unrefracting lens of God's Providence. "Sincere are all the words of my mouth," says Proverbs, "no one of them is wily or crooked; all of them are plain to the man of intelligence, and right to those who attain knowledge" (8:8-10). This plainness, this clarity of things, appears to the "little ones," meaning the simple ones, to whom God reveals that which is hidden from the worldly wise and the calculatingly prudent.

Without simplicity—that is, disinterested cooperation with God in training and forming students—the teacher can be lured by all the false baits of self-interest or spurious philosophy. "The wise man has eyes in his head, but the fool walks in darkness" (Eccles. 2:14) — in many cases, tragically, thinking that the darkness is light. He gets tangled up in self-conceit, unaware that "the foolishness of God is wiser than man, and the weakness of God is stronger than men" (1 Cor. 1:25).

How, for example, can the Beatitudes with their shocking paradoxes be understood, except with the wisdom of God? Read or listen to the hopelessly muddled arguments for birth control, divorce, euthanasia, or unnatural acts, and recall St. Paul's judgment: "The wisdom of the flesh is hostile to God, for it is not subject to the law of God, nor can it be" (Rom. 8:7).

It would seem, then, that aberrations in education are defended in the name of learning and scholarship and enlightenment by an "eloquence of his tongue, in whom there is no wisdom" (Isa. 33:19).

How Wisdom Is Attained

To insist further on the necessity of wisdom for a good teacher is to belabor the obvious. When the ordinary mathematics or English or religion teacher is convinced of this virtue's importance and desires vaguely to be a "wise teacher" with the wisdom of God, how does he go about attaining this wisdom?

Without realizing it, he has already taken a first step, since, as Proverbs says, "The beginning of wisdom is: get wisdom" (4:7); that is, first desire it.

Strictly speaking, of course, wisdom cannot be "earned." Essentially, it is a gift of God that comes to the Christian teacher with his faith; and, even more, perhaps, with the virtue of love — that love that desires everything that God wants and as He wants it.

This desire motivates the "fear of the Lord" that the Scriptures, in another place, give as "the beginning of wisdom" (Prov. 9:10);

not a servile or a groveling fear but a loving reverence for the will of God and an energetic will to see that it is done.

Doing the will of God with the help of God is a possible method of attaining wisdom. The initiate in the spirit of wisdom recognizes that "wickedness is foolish and folly is madness" (Eccles. 7:25) and that to lead a good life "makes a man wise according to God, and expert in many things" (*Imitation*, I:4:2).

So, after all, it is not such a completely hopeless task to set about learning.

On the other hand, the beginning teacher should not expect to become another Solomon overnight. The pursuit of wisdom must be lifelong: "From your youth embrace discipline; thus will you find wisdom with graying hair" (Ecclus. 6:18-19 [Sir. 6:18]).

The reference to "graying hair" should not be cause for discouragement; even Jesus *grew* in wisdom and grace with God and man. Since the model for right living is, of course, Christ, who is "the power of God and the wisdom of God" (1 Cor. 1:20), the study of His life and the humble following in His footsteps enlighten the teacher in his own life and work.

The attainment implies, first of all, pursuit—active and vigorous pursuit.

Christ had to complain that "the children of this world, in relation to their own generation, are more prudent than the children of light" (Luke 16:8); when He recommended His followers to be "wise as serpents" (Matt. 10:16), He was recommending an imitation of the worldly wise not in their objectives and methods but in their energy and interest.

Young or new teachers, especially, must turn their enthusiasm to learning and, in their efforts, must profit from the wisdom of others. The beginner who attempts to depend solely on himself and his own inexperience will be long, and perhaps eventually unsuccessful, in winning the mark. Ecclesiasticus provides the new teacher with a handy little primer, one that is optimistic in what it promises and practical in its advice. It says:

> If you wish, you can be taught [wisdom]; if you apply your-self, you will be shrewd. If you are willing to listen, you will learn; if you give heed, you will be wise. Frequent the company of the elders; whoever is wise, stay close to him. ([Sir.] 6:32-35)

To be wise is an ideal—and ideals are not easily achieved. The beginning teacher will make mistakes, but he will learn from them.

As an addendum to Ecclesiasticus, he might note the word to the wise given in the *Imitation*:

> Those who are yet but novices and unexperienced in the way of the Lord, if they will not govern themselves by the counsel of discreet persons, will be easily deceived and overthrown.
>
> And if they will rather follow their own judgment than believe others who have more experience, their future is full of danger if they continue to be drawn from their own conceit. (III:7:2, 3)

Finally, nothing can substitute for prayer in the good teacher's pursuit of that essential virtue wisdom, for "all wisdom comes from the Lord and with him it remains forever" (Ecclus. [Sir.] 1:1).

Only in asking for wisdom will the teacher receive it.

2

Prudence

Government of a Prudent Man

If wisdom is the virtue that, by viewing the panorama of God's scheme of things, proposes right and useful ends for a Christian teacher, it is the virtue of prudence that focuses upon and establishes a hierarchy of the definite means necessary for him to achieve those ends.

A teacher who has a noble goal but is following a bumbling path to reach it can do himself, his fellow faculty members, and his students irreparable damage. This is one case where good intentions are not enough; lofty aims remain ineffectual and idealistic until they are approached by concrete means.

These means—that is, what ought to be done in particular cases—reveal themselves to the prudent man. We say that such a person has "common sense" or that he is "organized"; but, however we label his peculiar quality, it is that which "gives him knowledge of his way" (Prov. 14:8) and instructs him as to how he should proceed correctly in a specific situation.

Unlike the other virtues that have God as their object, the virtue of prudence has the government or direction of oneself as its object. (Ultimately, of course, God is its end, since the best government of oneself is that which brings one's actions into conformity with the will of God.)

This guide to correctness, prudence, is defined by Aristotle as the virtue of the practical reason governing human actions conformably with truth.

It would seem to be a rational virtue, one wherein acting depends largely upon knowing the facts, understanding how they are related and how such relationships affect action. And it is not surprising to note the scriptural references to it couched in the following terms: "He who gains *intelligence* is his own best friend; he who keeps *understanding* will be successful" (Prov. 19:8).

The "gaining of intelligence" and the "keeping of understanding" must not be barren. The *Imitation* warns that "Many make it more their study *to know* than *to live* well, therefore are they often deceived, and bring forth none, or very little fruit" (I:3:4); and the New Testament, in speaking of the Commandments, the indispensable rules for human activity, says: "Whoever *carries them out* and teaches them, he shall be called great in the kingdom of heaven" (Matt. 5:19).

In translating knowledge into action, the "truth" with which action "conforms" is in many respects more all-embracing than the "truth" as Aristotle knew it: it is rather the whole complex of Christian life in the light of Revelation that influences the "truly prudent who looks upon all earthly things as nothing that he may gain Christ" (Phil. 3:8). As the Judeo-Christian conception of wisdom differs from the wisdom of the world, so does the Christian virtue of prudence—and the difference, of course, is Christ.

Effects of Prudence in Teaching

Since, as we have pointed out, prudence has as its object the governing of oneself, it precedes the other virtues. Silence, kindness, justice, and all the other virtues of a good teacher that will be considered later on are really dictates of a prudent judgment.

"Discretion will watch over you [the teacher], understanding will guard you" (Prov. 2:11), not because discretion and understanding are a kind of magic but because they logically lead to the necessary virtues for effective teaching.

Prudence will, for example, dictate first that the teacher himself be prepared to do his job. To form the minds of puzzled, searching young souls is a tremendous responsibility, and the teacher must have the correct answers, the straight facts, and sound principles when they are required.

The Acts of the Apostles provides, in a few lines, a wonderful model for every teacher in the early Christian Apollos, who "had been instructed in the Way of the Lord, and being fervent in spirit, used to speak and teach carefully whatever had to do with Jesus" (18:25).

The word *carefully* reveals a world of prudence and suggests to every teacher what his own attitude should be with truth—a delicacy and precision born of continuous and ever-deepening study that scorns the easy, the platitudinous, or the downright wrong answer as a solution for his questioning students. "Shrewd men gain the crown of knowledge," says Proverbs (14:18); but, perhaps, the aphorism should have been continued: "with much study and effort."

General preparation for class is not enough. Prudence and experience underline the necessity of day-to-day preparation of classes. If the teacher knows exactly what he is supposed to be doing, he will cut his discipline problems in half, he himself will be more confident as a result, and an atmosphere of study with direction and purpose will have a good chance of developing.

Good teaching does not just happen; it is planned. Like the poem over which some poet has worked for days with meticulous care, employing that "art that conceals art," so the teaching of the planner or plotter in the classroom seems many times to be effortless. It is not.

However, even having a command of one's subject is not quite enough. All things that are good are not necessarily expedient; and the young teacher especially should prudently teach *what* he is supposed to. If he were, for example, to walk into an American literature class and announce that there *is* no American literature and that, therefore, "we will read the Russian short-story writers instead," he would be out of order—and, as Ecclesiasticus says, "The government of a prudent man is well ordered" ([Sir.] 10:1).

If he were to decide that he would teach music appreciation instead of algebra I, psychology instead of freshman religion, or the Civil War instead of the fall of the Roman Empire, chaos would soon be conspicuous, not only in the course syllabus but in classroom discipline as well.

Prudence would also dictate that teaching should be accommodated to the age, intelligence, and future careers of students. To have high standards, to challenge students with the best they can do, and to offer a well-rounded course are all admirable goals; but to give immature minds works for which they are intellectually unprepared, or perhaps innately incapable of grasping, is self-defeating as well as evidence of very bad judgment.

The teacher here is imprudently ignoring the student and is, rather, teaching a subject. The very frequency with which the caricature crops up of the absentminded professor who goes his own way while the students go theirs is proof enough that such teachers (amazingly enough) exist.

There is a time for the teaching of Dostoyevsky or calculus, but the prudent man reflects long and weighs the pros and cons carefully before, if ever, he attempts to teach them in a sophomore high school class.

Not only does the teacher have to prepare himself and know *what* to teach, but he must also (the most difficult feat) know *how* to teach. Many brilliant and potentially fine teachers have failed in the classroom through lack of some rather elementary dictate of prudence (as well as some very complex ones, of course).

One of the most important and characteristic qualities of the good teacher we might call "foresight." In a sense, I suppose, it might be said to stem from the same prudential judgment that dictates the importance of lesson preparation, but foresight is perhaps more general.

A single goal may have a limitless number of approaches: the best teacher is he who, after considering the various possibilities, has shrewdly and with foresight chosen the most effective means to attain his end.

To do so requires imagination, the ability to project into the future classroom situation like a chess player planning his attack. Such ability arises from intelligence and also from long, considerate mulling over of the whole business of teaching and methodology.

Through this remote preparation by contemplation, the teacher can avoid many pitfalls, like the king in the Gospel (Luke 14:31–32) who carefully considered his chances for victory before rushing off to face the enemy.

Common sense in teaching also points to the importance of the study and use of psychology in dealing with students. In his meditation for the Third Sunday after Pentecost, St. La Salle says: "The student should have prudent and vigilant guides, who have sufficient knowledge of the things of piety and of boys' defects, so as to lead them effectively to correct them."

The knowledgeable teacher is better able to direct students since he knows both their strengths and weaknesses, how they think and how they react. He realizes the importance of tact—that is, of not riding roughshod over adolescent sensibilities and thereby perhaps forever ruining any chance of helping them in the future.

The good teacher knows when to smile and when to frown, when to be silent and when to speak, when to "crack down" and when to be lenient, and a thousand other "whens" that he will encounter *while* teaching (and that the best preparation cannot always foresee), the choice of alternatives all being based on study, circumspection, experience, and consideration of time, place, and manner of acting.

Some Cautions

On the subject of precautions for the young teacher, every writer could draw up a different list from that of every other writer, but each would probably be in agreement that the very nature of prudence makes *haste* a fundamental vice. The *Imitation* says, "It is great wisdom not to be rash in our doings" (I:4:2); this attitude is especially wise in a teacher.

If he is to act prudently, he might need to be informed of more facts than he has at hand, or he might need to take counsel—either necessity precluding rash decisions, which can only lead to regret for the teacher and damage to the student.

It is the precipitant act by a teacher who fails to take into account essential elements in a situation that can destroy a teacher-pupil relationship or spell trouble for an administration.

Rarely is a teacher sorry that he stifled his anger, held back a spontaneously bitter word, or did not give that blow across the face.

The opposite vice may be just as bad. A teacher suffering from an acute case of abulia—an inability to make a decision—may soon discover that it is not he but the students who are running the class. From exasperation with an indecisive teacher, students may well develop, at best, an attitude of reluctant toleration for the teacher—and the discipline necessary for teaching flies out the window.

Many situations require *rapid* decisions, but rapid decisions are not necessarily hasty. A rapid analysis of a critical moment may still be based upon a sound evaluation, a quick weighing of the elements entering into it, and a correct decision.

But such decisions depend on habits of prudence. After all, prudence *is* a virtue, and a virtue *is* a good *habit*. If the teacher habitually makes considered judgments, he is not likely to "muff it" at the unexpected crisis.

Another corroding vice opposed to prudence is one that might be called vincible ignorance of teaching procedures. We have already mentioned the importance of remote and proximate preparations for teaching, but there is also a neglect of knowledge of those disciplinary techniques that can mean success or failure.

One young teacher, amid the hail of study-period paper wads, chalk, and erasers, was known to take out his rosary and start whispering Hail Marys. Prayer is an essential catalyst in a well-run class, but on this occasion, it was hardly the appropriate answer to the situation.

Inconstancy is another bugbear for young teachers. Prudence requires a teacher to be consistent in his policy, or there is no policy. Once he has established certain legitimate rules and regulations, after seeing their necessity, he must stick to them.

If his decisions are maintained at certain times and not at others, students become confused and will inevitably rebel—and the teacher has no one to blame but himself for the scuttling of his classes. If he vacillates between softness and harshness, for example, he will alienate his whole class. And no teacher has ever tried to fight a whole class and won.

Finally, prudence is *not* cunning. Students will respond in most cases to prudent decisions; they are surprisingly rationalistic and, therefore, amenable to reasonable discipline. But they are rightly distrustful of trickery or slyness.

Learning Prudence

Most of these pedagogic precepts are generated by common sense. And a popular truism runs: Common sense cannot be taught. This is an easy generalization that, for the most part, is happily false; at least it is when the young teacher has the initial prudence to be docile toward his principal, advisers, and books.

Even these are intended not to solve his problems for him but rather to provide him with guidelines while he is still learning. They cannot, nor should they, make all prudential judgments for him, keeping him an intellectual minor for his whole life; rather, they educate him to make mature decisions for himself.

"The fool spurns his father's admonition," says Proverbs, "but prudent is he who heeds reproof" (15:5). The inexperienced teacher does well to follow direction carefully as he progresses through the first years in the classroom, if he ever intends to grapple by himself with his own problems.

He will also learn through experience (that "hard teacher")—not becoming amorally pragmatic, doing "what works," but basing his methodology on firm principles, experimenting, and wisely learning from trial and error what is right.

First in importance, he will learn prudence in prayer, since it is in this way that the Christian teacher's methods are brought into conformity with his goals.

After he has done everything that he himself can do, he must then trust in Providence—not being too anxious, not being too fearful, since inordinate anxiety or fear can destroy the disinterested work of prudence and replace it with the goal of personal success.

Rather, he should remember Christ's admonition: "Why are you fearful, O you of little faith?" (Matt. 8:26) and trust that Providence will come to the aid of prudence.

3

Piety

For Piety's Sake

Fleeing the flames of a crumbling Troy, "Pius Aeneas" (in Virgil's great Roman epic), carrying the venerated household gods, bearing upon his back his father, Anchises, and leading his son, Ascanius, by the hand, set out at the command of the gods to found the city of Rome.

In this famous literary tableau, the poet fixed for all time one of the most powerful images of piety known to man, and piety on its several levels: religious, filial, and patriotic. No wonder the early Fathers of the Church marveled at Virgil as a kind of pagan prophet of Christianity.

And yet the stoic Aeneas cannot really be identified with Christian piety, for there is a difference between the pagan's dogged devotion to his duty and the Christian's loving fulfillment of God's will—superficially the same, but essentially unlike one another.

Of no other virtue, perhaps, is the source or motivation as essential to its purity as that of piety.

Piety is not a popular virtue today, and to call someone "pious" has, unfortunately, pejorative suggestions of simplemindedness or scrupulosity or gullible sentimentality or plain hypocrisy. It is important, therefore, to understand just what it really is, what is its basis, and what is its authentic expression.

The term *piety* designates primarily a sentiment of love and respect for God. It is really synonymous with *religion* and governs all of man's worship that is directed to the Divinity; as such, it should be the ruling principle of his entire life, since man's whole life should be offered in worship to God.

Man is completely dependent on God for everything; sheer justice requires that he recognize this fact by voluntarily returning everything he has received to Him. St. Thomas, with habitual perspicuity, associated the gift of piety with the virtue of justice.

The Christian teacher, in justice, cannot permit the rights of God and those of his fellow men to be ignored; he does not rest until all these rights are fully respected; hungering and thirsting after justice, he is prepared to make any sacrifice to give this elementary expression of his love of God and his brothers in Christ.

But although fraternal, filial, and patriotic piety or justice (what is due to brothers, members of the family, and country) are subsumed under the term *piety*, it is most specifically, as we have said before, in man's giving to God directly His due that we use the term by itself today. In this sense, piety is the moral virtue of religion wherein, through our complete dependence, Faith enlightens us in regard to just *what* our duties to God are, and love inspires us as to *how* we can perform them with the greatest perfection.

The Teacher's Duty of Piety

Every teacher's practice of piety or religion has a peculiar ambivalence: both his God and his students bear silent witness to his acts; in *being* a practical, living example of Christian piety, the teacher as teacher best gives God His due and provides students with an ideal of piety to emulate. But, anomalously, when the teacher turns his eyes away from God and looks at himself to see whether he is being an example to the students, his piety becomes calculation, and he fails on both counts—as dutiful creature and living example.

The teacher's religious "edification" of students must be the overflow from his own genuine religious activity. As the teacher builds his own spiritual "edifice," block by spiritual block, the student, like a child following directions with construction toys, will build his own in mimic manner. "Let us practice before their eyes," says St. La Salle, "what we are trying to teach them. We will make a greater impression on them by a wise and modest conduct than by a multitude of words" (Meditation for the Second Sunday after Easter).

A teacher is, in this respect, for inspiration alone.

In a thousand ways, he reveals to his students every day the depth and reality of his devotion to God.

Most obvious is his own attitude toward class prayers. If his own vocal prayers in the morning, during the day, or at the end of the day are leisured, distinct, and thoughtful, so will the students' be. If he obviously considers the class prayers to be a necessary reminder of God in the midst of classes (and not, rather, an interference with "more important" things, such as biology or business), students also will. If the recitation of the Rosary (sometimes called the "apostolate of noise"—an appropriate designation derived from the general mumbling that accompanies it) or the celebration of the Holy Sacrifice of the Mass is attentively followed by the teacher, it will be by the student. If the name of God, the Most Blessed Virgin, and the saints are reverently pronounced, instruction of the best kind continues on.

The same holds for all the religious practices that fill the day, from the first Sign of the Cross (by the way, is the holy-water font filled?) through visits to chapel and the final prayers after school.

The external rites and manifestations of our worship of God are not, of course, the principal matter for the virtue of piety. They have meaning only to the degree to which they serve to express interior religion; otherwise, they would be the worst kind of formalism. The *Imitation* warns us that "if we place our progress in religion in these outward observances only, our devotion will quickly be at an end" (I:11:4).

But man is still man, with a body and with senses, and not a pure spirit; and only the ultrasophisticated or madly unrealistic could fail to see the practical use of external forms, if only to keep him attentive to the internal.

Furthermore, our body as well as our spirit is dependent on God, so why should it not join with the soul in saying thanks? The gesture of the Sign of the Cross or the genuflection or the vocal prayer can either help to sustain a religious sentiment or develop it. The symbol specifies the thought, fixes it, and sometimes even awakens it.

The child, for example, who identifies whispering with situations of awe or respect and who is taught to whisper in church may someday begin to realize *why* he whispers; he bows before a statue of the Blessed Virgin, learns respect for the Mother of God, and eventually learns *why* she deserves this respect.

Symbols *can* help in both private and public prayers: for example, kneeling at the bedside to say one's evening prayers is certainly not essential, but just as certainly it is an act helpful to piety (recalling to whom one is speaking and why) and perseverance in the practice of night prayer.

While the teacher realizes that the essence of prayerful homage is interior, he must accept the necessity of reverence in the external forms, especially for the students who, in their early spiritual development, have not as yet learned to do without them and may too frequently judge the interior by the exterior.

Perhaps men who teach are most guilty of inadvertently allowing the forms to lapse, failing to realize the importance of them for their students, uninitiated into the spiritual life.

No matter how proficient in prayer he becomes, he can never do without public prayer in any case. Besides the dangers of vagueness and indefiniteness that may develop in private worship, there is the impossibility of *extending* in private worship God's glory, unless it is externalized in some way.

Public prayer—that is, liturgical prayer—is religion par excellence: it is the Church praying as she did from the earliest times; as when, St. Luke tells us, upon Christ's triumphal entry into Jerusalem, "the whole company began to rejoice and to praise God with a loud voice" (19:37), or when St. Paul, after preaching to his congregation, "knelt down and prayed with them all" (Acts 20:36).

The most perfect act of public piety is not just a prayer but an action, a sacrifice—the most ancient symbol by which a man can acknowledge his dependence on God—the offering of some external goods. And the summit of all human religion is the only perfect sacrifice, the sacrifice of Christ in the Holy Mass. The most perfect private prayer could not approach the infinitely satisfying offering of the Body and Blood of Christ.

It is, then, by both private and public manifestations of an interior and wholehearted submission to God that a teacher attains and exercises piety.

Impiety

Good teachers are pious teachers; but call a teacher, especially a man, "pious" and it's a "fighting word."

Why?

Unfortunately, aberrations that parade under the colors of piety have given it a bad name: it has taken on the sickly pale tinge of a man with a mushy heart or softening brain or flabby muscles.

There is nothing offensive or effeminate about authentic piety; rather, as we have seen, it is a virile virtue requiring a sound mind (that honestly sees where man's strength lies—in God—and humbly thanks Him for it) and a loving heart (that sees the good, desires it, and aggressively strives to attain it).

A man can never possess too much devotion; but external acts can be inclined to excess when they are directed toward irrelevant ends; for example, when, either through ignorance or unrestrained emotion, a teacher's practices verge on the superstitious.

Unwarranted claims of power for certain medals, novenas, prayers, badges, or images are presumptuous temptations of God rather than evidences of faith; they are particularly dangerous since all of these pious practices, when understood correctly, *are* useful and, in submission to God's will, effective. The unwary teacher has simply misused them.

Another distortion of devotion occurs when the teacher tries to be "holier than the Church" and holds on to outmoded rites, letting externals take precedence over spiritual religion.

An example of such a travesty of piety would be continued devotion to a "saint" after the Church has suppressed or recommended a de-emphasis of such devotion or a failure to enter into a manner of devotion (for example, continuing use of pious prayers rather than the use of the missal at Holy Mass) suggested by the Church.

In most of these cases, the damage is done by overemphasizing private devotions and failing to recognize the importance of liturgical prescriptions and of their wise interpretation and the necessity of conformity to these rites. Popularity of a devotion cannot supplant the Church's approval, and the truly pious teacher should, like the Church, be chary of the dangerous practice of propagating cults based on apparitions, revelations, prophecies, and miracles.

Imagine the damage done to a child who has been stirred up to a devotion that is based on a fraud (false visions or rose petals from Heaven).

The sentimental can be carried over into art and music. The pictures and statues of an effeminate Christ or a masculine Madonna, in baby blue, pink, and gilt, perpetuate the worst visual atrocities of nineteenth-century art.

Music should be an overflowing of the soul that invites all the sensible powers to chant a homage of heart to God—not to self in the form of an emotional catharsis.

While ignorance is an explanation for these grotesque aberrations from piety in art and music, it is not an excuse for them.

Perhaps as bad as the "overpious"—and frequently going along hand in hand with it—is the teacher who perpetrates a picture of piety as undiluted gloom and unhappiness. Thanks, but the students won't have any. They may even become allergic to a teacher's sound practices if he makes religion repulsive by overdoing it.

This type of teacher may be so encumbered with pious practices that it is a kind of three-ring circus for him to "get them all in," and he develops anxieties from his superstitious belief that numbers are what is important: he is the inveterate counter of aspirations ("I said four thousand aspirations today") and the fanatic tabulator of "indulgences gained."

Since both aspirations and indulgences are good, the danger of making a fetish of them rather than a pious practice is all the more grave.

In all the references to prayer and devotion in the Scriptures, words such as *joy*, a *glad* heart, and *song* are used. St. James says, "Is any one of you sad? Let him pray. Is any one in good spirits? Let him sing a hymn" (5:13). Proverbs says, "A glad heart lights up the face" (15:13), and the Psalms, "Sing praise to our God, for he is gracious; it is fitting to praise him" (146 [147]:1).

Where here is gloom? Where the "numbers game"? Where is the grubbing about in formalism?

Certainly, to "look gloomy like the hypocrites" (Matt. 6:16) will only turn the student away from joyful and loving devotion to God and His work.

The error opposed to sentimentality, but one just as dangerous, is insensitivity to spiritual things. Teaching men are perhaps more frequently guilty of this error than of sentimentalism. Mistaken as to the nature of what constitutes masculine piety and overzealous to avoid a falsely feminine piety, they may verge dangerously upon the irreverent—toward prayer, the very name of God, and practice.

Carelessness of posture or pronunciation during prayers in class or at Mass will be reflected in the indifference of the student to prayer; lightness in acts such as the Sign of the Cross or genuflection will be presumed by the students to mirror interior irreverence.

Students learn more by example than by instruction, so example must be given with care.

Teaching Piety, an Act of Piety

If piety is the offering of homage and service to God, the best act of piety a teacher can perform is his work itself—teaching.

Teaching the true nature of piety is itself a profoundly pious activity. Such teaching involves not only the formal study of the truths of religion so that the truth may be taught, but also the practice of moral virtues so that the life, based upon truth, may be lived.

The Christian teacher, living his life in this manner, offers a life of perpetual piety and fulfills the command of Christ to "pray at all times" (Luke 21:36).

4

Zeal

Have Zeal for God

St. Thérèse, the Little Flower, said before her death that she would spend her Heaven doing good on earth. And during her life in the secluded Carmelite cloister, she devoted herself to prayer and sacrifice for the missionaries in distant lands.

On the other hand, St. Francis Xavier, the great Jesuit missionary to India and Japan in the sixteenth century, left his home and country to perform veritable miracles of conversion.

But both were militant, zealous apostles fired by the Holy Ghost's spirit of love.

Every Christian must, like St. Thérèse and St. Francis, be an apostle, whether he dons sandals on a Chinese sampan or "cultivates his little plot of ground" at home.

St. Jean-Marie Vianney, the Curé of Ars, considered a kind of naive incompetent by some of his contemporaries, made the confession box his apostolate; St. John Bosco, the founder of the Salesians, with joyful simplicity taught abandoned children and young people how to love God; and St. La Salle, the great teacher of teachers, turned his back on a comfortable canonry, "sold all that he had, gave it to the poor," and dedicated his life to teaching the neglected waifs who "roamed the streets in packs."

All of these heroes of the Church shared in the Pentecostal fire that burned in St. Peter when, receiving the Holy Ghost, he went out of fearful seclusion to preach and to baptize three thousand souls in one day.

Every good teacher must share in this universally Christian spirit of apostolicity that we call zeal. Zeal leads him to try, with great love and devoted energy, to further God's glory and to take all the steps conducive to this end.

For the Christian teacher, the first function of zeal must be, according to St. La Salle, "to procure the salvation of the children confided to his care." This is the teacher's apostolate, his mission.

His "missionary activities" in the classroom are *after* his own perfection but *not apart* from it, the very essence of his vocation as a Christian teacher.

Apostolic Action

"If it doesn't move, it's dead." Activity is the sign of life, and the very kind of movement of life expresses what is most specific and most personally vital about it: What are its aims and objects? Toward what does it move?

The sunflower stretches toward the sky; the lion roams about, seeking whom it may devour; the scholar searches for truth and translates it into humane uses. The Christian seeks the vision of God. But God is grasped best, human life being what it is and needing a personal inspiration, in Christ, who came to save the world. By Christ, through Christ, with Christ, the Christian teacher explores the world of human personality that Christ so loved and reclaims it for Him.

This is the activity by which the Christian teacher is both characterized and recognized.

A teacher who is not interested in teaching is a contradiction. If he has the love of God and a high ideal, he must express both through striving, through an effort to bring all men to God, especially the students who come within his sphere.

A physician unconcerned about medicine, or a lawyer oblivious of court decisions, would be not only unsuccessful but also a fool. A Christian teacher who believes salvation to be the most important thing in life for all and who huddles his knowledge in his own arms is a rather flimsy excuse for a teacher.

Good tends to diffuse itself, and the greatest good should certainly be propagated.

If wisdom reveals man's destination, and prudence charts his course, zeal is the steam of love that starts up the engine; otherwise, stasis sets in, and nothing happens. "He does much," says the *Imitation*, "who loves much" (I:15:2).

Love of God, then, is the reservoir of zeal.

It cannot be artificially manufactured. The zeal that works for the salvation of the student must be the overflow of the zeal by which the teacher seeks to perfect himself in the love of God. As such, it is meaningful exertion, not merely fortuitous movement.

Ambition versus Zeal

Natural ambition sometimes paints itself to look like zeal but rarely passes for it, since its aim is selfish.

Popularity, self-satisfaction, success with an administration, faculty, or public — in short, the balms to pride — provide the merely ambitious teacher with his rewards. But the *Imitation* warns: "He that has true and perfect charity seeks himself in no one thing, but desires only the glory of God in all things" (I:15:3).

Lucifer and the archangel Michael were both great apostles, fired with zeal — but one was out for himself, the other for God.

Nor is true zeal always measured by evident success. The timid, the reticent, the inept, the unprepossessing, or perhaps just the insecure or vulnerable new teacher may have the desire and the energy that characterize the zealous, without any of the accomplishment, while the flamboyant extrovert with a flair for the flashy may seem to win the show hands down.

But zeal is not obtrusive: it need not do great things; it need do just the ordinary things greatly.

In fact, it is well for the new and idealistic teacher, filled with the exuberance of youth, to watch himself carefully in order to avoid the hectic, short-lived enthusiasm that goes off in a thousand directions at once and soon gets bored with the monotony of necessary and unspectacular duties or gets frustrated with measured success.

Zeal is a flame; but it should burn low, steadily, intensely; it should not be a momentary, if hot and brilliant, blast.

If the teacher dissipates his energies in restless, pointless pursuits, he will eventually, when distractions cloy, feel the emptiness of his activities.

Natural freshness and enthusiasm can, of course, be of great aid in reclaiming the worst misfits in a school and, with good direction and purity of intention, can do immeasurable good. The spiritual is, after all, often built on the natural.

Nor should the fact that success is not necessarily a measure of a young teacher's zeal be his excuse for inertia.

Students are more often led along by admiration for what a teacher *is* than for what he *knows* or even for what he *teaches*.

Since personality is so important, a young teacher should try to develop those traits that so easily inspire hero worship in potentially idealistic adolescents: he should be interested in what they are interested in — batting averages or astronauts; he should encourage their stumbling steps in the intellectual life — low IQs as well as budding geniuses; he should "like" his students — in a genuine, manly manner—for only in so doing can he really work *with* the students rather than talk *at* them.

Zeal without love and effort is a delusion and a dead end. As St. La Salle says:

> Your zeal would have little or no success if it were limited to words; to make it effective, your example must reinforce your teaching. It will become perfect if you practice what you preach; then it will make a real impression on the students, who are inclined to imitate rather what they see done than to practice what we tell them. (Meditation for August 13)

Test of Zeal

Zeal that is not obedient and moderated is fanaticism.

It is inordinate in a very *literal* sense, since it actually destroys order. Obedient zeal, on the other hand, serves as a channel through which God's grace and peace flow; it is *well ordered*, leading to the fulfillment first of those things that are of duty and major importance.

If the teacher neglects the preparation of his lessons or if he neglects his own spiritual development (perhaps skipping prayer) in favor of some extracurricular activity of his own choosing (anything from coaching baseball to directing a chorus), he is lacking in a sense of proportion that is primary: first things first.

If he fails to do his job thoroughly, to keep at it steadily despite difficulties or failure, or to organize his work so that it gets somewhere, he fails doubly. "He does much that does *well* what he does," says the *Imitation* (I:15:2).

But once a teacher has been assigned a job, then he will canalize his zeal to do it well.

A high school principal wants a teacher to run his own classes with intelligence and responsibility. Cooperation with administration should not be interpreted as paralysis of will and a chance to dump all problems in the principal's office.

After the limits of a project or a teaching schedule have been defined, an alert teacher will be relied upon to apply all necessary natural and supernatural means to complete the work independently of further supervision.

The question sometimes arises: If zeal is related to the "salvation of the students' souls," how does teaching agreement of subjects and predicates in English or non-Euclidean geometry or the anatomy of an earthworm figure in?

True zeal can find an outlet in any type of work. Teachers of such different subjects as literature, history, and mathematics have countless opportunities to infuse sound religious values during the work of any class.

Reflections and interpretations must and do color the instructions of a zealous and alert teacher, no matter what the subject.

But besides the incidental opportunities, however real, for injecting a spiritual note occasionally, and the general influence on the students of the teacher's example and attitude toward life, a teacher is effective in zeal when he communicates a reverence for the truth and gives the students a sound preparation for taking their proper places in society.

They must work out their salvation in the world, must be prepared to do a good job with integrity, and must be taught to see the relationship between their own work and their own salvation.

The teacher's pursuit of truth is, in the long run, more effective zeal than irrelevant "pieties" could possibly be.

When the young teacher has done all that he can, by way of personal development, inspiration, preparation, and example, he must, like St. Paul, thank God for any measure of success he is able to muster, since it is He, after all, who "gives the increase," if there is any (1 Cor. 3:6). Without Him, the teacher can do nothing.

Such teachers are Christian apostles, like those first ones, of whom St. Mark says, "They went forth and preached everywhere, while the Lord worked with them and confirmed their preaching by the signs that followed" (16:20).

The signs may not be immediately forthcoming, but, as St. La Salle consoled his young teachers, "The principles of a good education always remain in the soul and sooner or later assert themselves" (Meditation for October 15).

Generosity

All Brave and Many Generous

Those little onion-like Chinese balls, intricately carved one within another out of ivory and patience, provide an apt symbol for the relationship between the virtue of generosity and the other virtues: wisdom, contained at the core and enveloped by love, must find expression in zeal for salvation of souls; but zeal, in turn, expands with joy to exercise itself generously.

Generosity, then, whether it be natural or supernatural, is essentially a willingness to sacrifice oneself for others; it is a social virtue *extraordinaire*, since it leads the teacher to act with spontaneous sympathy, not calculating the gain or loss but desiring only the good of those with whom he comes into contact.

The generous teacher is magnanimous — literally the man with a great soul that embraces all of his students and wants to do all good for them, certainly an ambitious venture.

Why?

Because the teacher realizes that the student has a tremendous value per se. Not merely human friendship but a love based on the vision of youths as sons of God, sharing God's divine life, inspires the teacher to help them beyond the call of duty, to help them to realize that potential life within themselves.

The teacher sees more clearly than his students do their essential nobility and possibilities, and he selflessly helps to mold them. Adolescents are involved in all sorts of contingencies and necessities of life on earth: human needs such as earning tuition, solving moral problems, adjusting to society, and understanding their own mixed-up physical, emotional, and spiritual lives.

Therefore, they must be "structured," taught to see themselves as the more objective teacher can, arranging all of those distracting or jumbled elements to the service of an immortal soul.

Generosity always implies giving up something, perhaps one's own comfort or wages or advancement, for the sake of a higher or greater good — in this case, the good being God's service and the action becoming sacrifice (made sacred by the offering of it to God, the highest possible Good).

Like zeal, therefore, generosity is the concomitant of vision, the practical projection of idealism.

It is a youthful virtue: young countries (such as America) and young people (such as novices and seminarians and first-year teachers) are noted for the wholehearted way in which they take on jobs, assume tasks that are not within the strict requirement of duty, and are always ready to volunteer to take a class or scrub a floor, nothing being too much trouble for them.

They find actual happiness in self-sacrifice, not as a kind of masochism that enjoys suffering for its own sake but as the comparatively paltry price of a great objective — a realization of the brotherhood of man or the fellowship of God.

The young Christian teacher who has glimpsed what God has generously given to him wants to act with like generosity toward others. He is eager to give freely what he has freely received.

Everyone is vaguely aware that this is true about teachers. Even on a natural level, it was the basis for the notorious practice over many years for teachers to be crassly underpaid, since, as the shrewd exploiters of idealism averred, "their reward was in the great work they are doing."

If sacrifice through the humanist's ideal is possible, how much richer should it be for the *Christian* humanist. By a kind of paradox, when he begins to love God exclusively, he becomes the exclusive property of all, like St. Paul, who says, "Free though I was as to all, unto all I have made myself a slave that I might gain the converts" (1 Cor. 9:19).

Effects of Generosity

A teacher's spirit of generosity, if based on supernatural motives, will have very concrete effects on his work, some relating to his attitude toward himself and some relating to his attitude toward his students. If he is disinterestedly looking for the good of the students rather than his own, he will never be guilty of subordinating the student to his own advantage. As St. Paul says, "I myself in all things please all men, not seeking what is profitable to myself but to the many, that they may be saved" (1 Cor. 10:33).

He will, for example, put aside purely personal studies when they interfere with those necessary for teaching well. College and university degrees are good things (indeed, they are indispensable today) and, in the long run, represent knowledge that should contribute to good teaching; but if a teacher were to neglect his classes for the pursuit of scholastic prestige, or perhaps just for the satisfaction of his own curiosity or interest (both, of course, good in themselves), he would not be doing his job.

Similarly, if direct orders were necessary to keep him from withdrawing into his ivory tower when he should be prefecting a lunch period or teaching a class, he could hardly be labeled as even just, let alone generous, in his service. Rather, the generosity of the teacher should be *voluntary*, not forced, both giving services when they are requested by administrators or students and even offering them when they are not asked for.

If possible, service should be given *cheerfully*.

Generosity is a gift of something not required; and a gift given in duty, through social form or pressure, is no gift at all.

God is not the only one who likes a "cheerful giver." Where the patronizing, the officious, the merely "just" teacher repels, the cheerfully generous teacher attracts, rendering service so unobtrusively and painlessly that the one served is the object of the attention rather than the one serving or even the service itself. The old cliché about attracting more flies with a spoonful of honey than a barrelful of vinegar has a certain appropriateness here.

The truly generous teacher does not expect gratitude for what he so willingly offers. "When you have done your duty well, expect no reward on earth," says St. La Salle (Meditation for August 13). Students, it is true, can sometimes be rather ungrateful or thoughtless little monsters of selfishness, accepting extra help and services, even demanding them, without so much as a "thank you." But if, in such a case, a teacher requires thanks, he must be sure that he does so for the good of forming the student and not merely through personal pique.

Material repayment in the way of gifts, invitations to dinner, and so forth can be doubly dangerous, leading either to favoritism shown toward the children of the affluent or to downright compromise of one's standards when confronted by the necessity of reciprocating favors with the only thing one has to reciprocate with—marks.

Furthermore, the idealism of a teacher can withstand very little bribery; soon the "golden goals" that led him into teaching will be dimmed, and trouble will start.

The generous teacher also learns to pardon offenses when he can do so without injury to his authority.

Realizing that students are still in the formative stage, hotheaded, frequently and irrationally rebellious, and victims of their own quixotic temperaments, the teacher knows when to be magnanimous and when to punish.

Sometimes he must discipline, of course, for the good of the student, although it might mean that, at least temporarily, he will be unpopular. Even St. Paul had to say, "I will most gladly spend and be spent myself for your souls, even though, *loving you more, I be loved less*" (2 Cor. 12:15).

Perhaps the principal characteristic of a teacher's generosity will be its universality. Since its basis is the dignity and value of every student in the eyes of God, it embraces each and every student, rising above natural sympathies and dominating instinctive antipathies.

Again, like St. Paul, such a teacher can say, "I became all things to all men, that I might save all. I do all things for the sake of the gospel, that I may be made partaker thereof" (1 Cor. 9:22-23).

Unless a teacher makes this effort of supernatural orientation, his apostolate is limited and ineffective. Timid students, for example, are easily overlooked in the shuffle, while the bold ones are disciplined and "put in their place."

On the other hand, since it is so natural to want to see results, a teacher may be lured into the trap of teaching almost exclusively the gifted student or the good worker or the alert one. These should all profit from the generous challenges of an imaginative teacher, but he need not neglect the slow or the inattentive. In fact, he probably needs to work harder for them, knowing that the rewards will be meager or nonexistent. One is sometimes tempted to put a bomb (metaphorically speaking) under the lazy student to get him moving—but bombs have a nasty tendency to destroy instead of develop.

Every student should therefore be the object of a teacher's generosity, although its expression will undoubtedly take different forms for different students. "It should be one of the principal cares of those engaged in teaching, to know all their students and how to deal with each of them," says St. La Salle (Meditation for the Second Sunday after Easter).

Some Problems Related to Generosity

To talk about problems regarding generosity is inexact. The real problem is how to keep up one's generosity throughout a whole lifetime of teaching.

As we have noted before, generosity seems to be almost connatural with youth; but something sometimes happens to the first fine glow.

What accounts for the sputtering out of that brave new flame?

The most obvious reason for its short life is that what at times passes for generosity is not really generosity at all but a soothing self-delusion. A young teacher may be simply following his own bent, complacently doing what comes naturally, taking up extra work that carries with it praise or credit, or assuming (because restless activity is congenial to the high spirits of beginning teachers) that *external* labors are the more important ones.

Such self-duplicity is a two-edged sword. The lazy or selfish teacher may hide his negligence of duty under a superciliously pure attitude about the dirty, nonacademic jobs, maintaining that the hierarchy of educational objectives precludes getting one's hands dirty with extracurriculars.

No one, except the teacher himself, will ever know for sure if he is generous or merely deluded; but if his generosity is to be measured, he should ask himself whether he is doing what *God* wants or what *he* wants. With this criterion, he should be able to decide, at least about himself.

He could also check by asking himself if his generosity is limited by time (when it is convenient for him), by place (in one school and not another), by type of work (not directed by the principal but by personal choice). The "no time" and "not my job" excuses for avoiding work should be discarded.

A second obstacle to persevering generosity is an almost physical one: natural vigor, satisfaction, or emotion. Virtually every first-year teacher dedicates himself to the self-surrender of teaching on an initial wave of enthusiasm. But emotion ebbs, and the enthusiast is left disconsolately stranded on the teaching shores. Generosity begins to look rather bleak, the work to seem unreasonable.

Soon he is arguing with himself that he needs "a little relaxation every now and then," or he wants to go to a school where he will be "appreciated," where he will not be casting his pearls before swine. The way is opened for his getting involved with trifles of self-interest—and generosity soon flickers out, extinguished in self-pity.

If generosity is erroneously identified with a flurry of reckless activity, the passage of years, which carries with it an inevitable decrease in sheer physical stamina and energy, will signal an accompanying decrease in "generosity"; but if it has been solidly grounded on faith and love, the gift of mind and heart—which is the only true generosity—should be ever greater.

True generosity will grow if the teacher, like St. Paul, keeps his sights trained upon Christ's example: He gave His whole life and, for thanks, was nailed to the Cross. A teacher must be generous if he remembers this example of supreme generosity and the invitation that went with it: "If anyone wishes to come after me, let him deny himself, and take up his cross daily, and follow me" (Luke 9:23).

With his eye on Christ, the generous teacher can echo the prayer of St. Francis:

Lord, make me an instrument of Thy peace.
Where there is hatred, let me sow love;
Where there is injury, pardon;
Where there is doubt, faith;
Where there is despair, hope;
Where there is darkness, light;
Where there is sadness, joy.
O Divine Master, grant that I may not so much
seek to be consoled, as to console;
To be understood, as to understand;
To be loved, as to love;
For it is in giving that we receive;
It is in pardoning that we are pardoned;
And it is in dying that we are born to eternal life.
Amen.

6

Justice

The Just Live Forever

Christ warned all of His disciples that their justice should exceed that of the scribes and the Pharisees, those living handbooks of social injustice. But to Christian teachers, His injunction is especially meaningful, since justice, that virtue by which they give everyone what is his due in strict equality, is essential to their success in any educational system.

Students are quick to sense and slow to forgive a teacher who violates the rules of fair play. The very term *fair play* connotes a certain beauty, a loveliness born of order and proportion; and the teacher risks being a "foul ball" when he plays fast and loose in the game of education. An innate sense of justice seems to exist in most students, and with it they weigh the teacher in the balance. They may overlook one who is poorly prepared or naturally ungifted, but the hue and cry will be raised: "He was wrong" (for *wrong*, read *unjust*), when he unreasonably or passionately dispenses with the dictates of simple justice in the classroom.

Justice and Discipline

Ninety percent of the problem regarding justice has to do with a teacher's establishing of order in the classroom. Of course, there must be order, and discipline is one of the means to bring it about;

but the teacher should never confuse the one for the other: order is not necessarily discipline, nor discipline order.

In the class where students are sitting at military attention, with hands folded, backs rigid, and voices hushed, order may reign, but it may be a sterile "other-directed" order that is uncongenial for learning. Ideally, discipline should be self-discipline guided by the wise teacher, not an imposed discipline enforced with military tactics by an overbearing, petty tyrant.

This does not mean that unbridled "permissiveness" is the correct approach to order in the classroom. Such an attitude is based on the assumption that students naturally do the correct thing. They do not, or they do so only rarely without coaching.

Ecclesiasticus says: "A colt untamed turns out stubborn, a son left to himself grows up unruly; pamper your child and he will be a terror for you, indulge him and he will bring you grief" ([Sir.] 30:8-9). Students must be led by rewards and correction, but unless both are inspired by justice, discipline will never hold sway.

Sometimes students must be punished for willful violations of reasonable rules: "Withhold not chastisement from a boy," says Proverbs (23:13).

Laxness can be as unjust as cruelty. But the teacher should consider first whether or not he could perhaps do more good for the recalcitrant student by invoking clemency than by meting out the full penalty.

If he decides that the action must be taken, he must make sure that "the punishment fits the crime" and that it is not excessively severe, vindictive browbeating, or cowing of defenseless adolescents guilty of minor misdemeanors.

Rash, that is, unreasonable, punishment—or even unreasonable rewards, for that matter—will create a spirit of rebellion or of criticism or of jealousy among the students.

Attitudes of the Just Teacher

Perhaps too much is said about a teacher's disciplining of students and not enough about respecting them. Christ Himself said: "See that you do not despise one of these little ones; for I tell you, their angels in heaven always behold the face of my Father in heaven" (Matt. 18:10). Skittish and annoying as students can be, they are still human beings to be reverenced and loved, not stones to be pounded into shape and arranged.

When a teacher pays just respect to students, the respect will frequently be mutual, and the problem of discipline is fairly well solved. In this way, one can avoid other pedagogic vices that are too common: name-calling (beneath the dignity of any sensible teacher), derision (a vulgar and easy shortcut to breaking a student's spirit), and sarcasm (the facile weapon of a sharp tongue dipped in gall).

The student has a right to his own self-respect and the respect of his fellow classmates. This right also extends to his good name among the faculty members — a right violated when teachers get together in bull sessions and gossip about students' failures or go so far as to spread their secret and serious faults among those who have no right to know them.

Respect for students will also require, in justice, that a teacher deal courteously with them. Pleasing words and actions (without overdoing them to the point of sycophancy or preciosity) mark a polite man; and students deserve a teacher's gentlemanliness.

Certain demands of decorum, of good usage in society, are not abrogated simply because they have young people as their object. They themselves appreciate simple courtesy and directness, since it is a recognition of their essential importance — a recognition that is, strictly speaking, their due.

As part of this "decorum," the teacher owes the students, above all, complete truthfulness in both language and action. A teacher who is shifty or double-dealing with his students is not only a moral delinquent but also a menace in the teaching profession, which is, ultimately, the profession that purports to communicate truth. Once he tampers with it, he is no longer a fit shepherd for his flock. "Anything deceitful the just man hates" (Prov. 13:5), and the teacher must be just in all things.

In justice, every teacher owes his class an impartial service, without consideration for age or ability or social status. An eighteen-year-old dolt in a freshman English class is as deserving as the high IQ with polished manners. The teacher who does not adapt himself to their needs without regard to his personal preferences does so to his own peril: he will soon be found out and labeled for what he is—an unjust steward of God's work.

Naturally, some students will attract and others repel; but, considered from a supernatural viewpoint, both kinds must be treated in the same way. "Teacher's pets" are rapidly discovered; and a class is soon divided, with the "pets" as well as the "others" walling the teacher out from his apostolate. "If you show partiality toward persons," say the Scriptures, "you commit sin" (James 2:9)—and pedagogic suicide, it might be added.

Unreasonable though he may feel the requirement to be, the teacher must also be uniform in his conduct in the classroom; at least he should try to be. And since justice is a virtue of the will, his will to be consistent is half the battle.

Some days, a natural feeling of euphoria resulting from a good night's sleep, a restful vacation, or just a bright day after rain can lead a teacher to loosen up on what he will allow students to get away with, while the next day a headache may dictate new and stringent fulminations that leave students in a perpetual state of confusion. Both the teacher's conduct in class and his daily routine should be consistent. They should not operate one day and not the next, nor should they apply to one student and not another. "Ups and downs" in any classroom will only turn it upside down eventually.

Informed Teachers

Such qualities as fairness, impartiality, and so forth must be demanded in justice of any teacher. However, perhaps nothing is as strongly dictated to him *qua* teacher by justice (indeed, as it is by prudence as well) as fidelity to the job itself of teaching, the fulfillment of the teacher's bargain to be a teacher: teaching the truth, what *should* be taught, and teaching it well.

In order to teach the truth, the teacher, in justice, must be prepared by education to teach. "Be informed before speaking," says Ecclesiasticus (18:18 [Sir. 18:19]). Goodwill in a teacher is fine, but an *informed* teacher with goodwill is necessary.

He has been contracted to teach, and he must fulfill that contract. "Look to the ministry which thou hast received in the Lord, that thou fulfill it," says St. Paul (Col. 4:17). A teacher who is poorly instructed or ignorant in his field is a scandal (in the strict meaning of the word), an understandable cause for discredit to his profession, and a source of untold harm to the students.

Justice further requires that even the informed teacher should disseminate his information with care, teaching what and how he should. St. La Salle, patron of all teachers, warned his young followers: "Your instructions should be understood by them [the students] and proportioned to their intelligence; otherwise, they would be of little use to them" (Meditation for the Second Sunday after Easter). A teacher indifferent to learning or to methodology fails fundamentally in his first and foremost obligation of justice to the students, while, on the other hand, "the just man's lips nourish many" (Prov. 10:21).

Even if social morality, involving as it does all of one's external acts that put a man into relationship with his neighbor, did not insist that teachers be just, the reward promised to the just man in the book of Wisdom would be sufficient encouragement for a teacher to exercise the virtue with rigor: "The just live forever, and in the Lord is their recompense, and the thought of them is with the Most High. Therefore shall they receive the splendid crown, the beauteous diadem, from the hand of the Lord—for he shall shelter them with his right hand, and protect them with his arm" (5:15–16).

7

Kindness

Kind Hearts Are More Than Coronets

Justice requires that students receive what is due to them *by right*; generosity offers service and sacrifice *voluntarily*; but it is kindness—the virtue that flows from the *heart* and leads the teacher to think of and to act toward the students as Christ would—that is of paramount importance for him, if he is to effect the greatest good in his students.

A cold and formal sacrifice and justice without warmth are possible; cold kindness, however, is inconceivable, since acts of kindness spring from love, in imitation of the acts of a loving Christ, who said, "Love one another, as I have loved you" (John 13:34).

Attitude is fundamental to kindness: action is a part of it, but action in itself is not enough. Lowell, in his *Vision of Sir Launfal*, has Christ say:

> Who gives *himself* with his alms feeds three—
> Himself, his hungering neighbor, and me.

A kindness, as a work of charity, must give from the soul, must be accomplished by a teacher's entering into a kind of spiritual union and sympathy with the student—in fact, by the understanding of *kind*ness in the sense that the Anglo-Saxons used the word.

Cynn, or *kin*, referred to members of the same race, family, or stock; and *kin* have special understanding of one another, simply because they share the same nature or boast a proud lineage. And what profounder kinship can there be than that between the teacher and the taught in the Mystical Body of Christ?

"As the body is one and has many members," says St. Paul, "and all the members of the body, many as they are, form one body, so also is it with Christ. For in one Spirit we were all baptized into one body … and we were all given to drink of one Spirit. And if one member suffers anything, all the members suffer with it, or if one member glories, all the members rejoice with it" (1 Cor. 12:12, 13, 26).

To suffer or to glory with the fellow members of the Mystical Body is to "be kind."

By the action of the Holy Ghost, teacher and student in the spiritual alchemy of charity become more than friends; they become brothers, one in Christ, and from this most perfect social awareness arises the familial kindness of love.

It is more than mere humanitarianism, which may be simply fellow feeling; it is based on Christ's illumination of social relationships: "As long as you did it for one of these, the least of my brethren, you did it for me" (Matt. 25:40).

Christian kindness extends, therefore, to works involving not only man's body but also his soul, the teacher recollecting Christ's words: "What shall it profit a man, if he gain the whole world and suffer the loss of his soul?" (Mark 8:36).

Characteristics of Kindness

Manner, not matter, best distinguishes a Christian kindness from the merely humanitarian deed. For one thing, it is specific, not generic, sympathizing with individual people, not abstract "humanity"; an example is Mary at the wedding feast of Cana, foreseeing the embarrassment of the host and hostess and quietly and kindly helping them out of their difficulty.

The teacher, like Mary, must learn to see the individual face in the amorphous "class," the individual problem in the "sea of troubles," if he is to do any good.

When he has focused his attention on the individual, he must, as Christ did, have compassion. And compassion is a suffering-with the erring or the distressed. It is not condolence of sin but pity for the inevitable consequences of it.

Sensitive to either bodily or mental anguish, the kind teacher attempts to forestall when he can a student's hurt and to soothe it when he cannot prevent it.

The compassionate Christ extended His comfort to both "the multitudes" and the individual sinner, with kindness looking to both their physical and spiritual needs. Students, unaccustomed to bearing pain, whether it is the result of the other students' insensitivity, of the normal family troubles — sickness, death, and finances — or of personal defects of body or character, need an understanding, Christlike teacher.

Understanding is a prelude to kindness, since kindness flows from love, and "we cannot love what we do not know." The axiom that "to understand is to forgive all" needs qualification, but there is a great measure of truth in it.

If a teacher is to forgive, like Christ, who said: "Blessed are the merciful, for they shall obtain mercy" (Matt. 5:7), he must try to see what makes a student act as he does and, understanding the springs of action, must give helpful, straight correction (a frequently necessary addendum to forgiveness) or consolation. "Let all bitterness, and wrath, and indignation, and clamor, and reviling, be removed from you, along with all malice," says St. Paul; "on the contrary, be kind to one another, and merciful, generously forgiving one another, as also God in Christ has generously forgiven you" (Eph. 4:31–32).

Allied to forgiveness is the quality of indulgence—a rather unsavory word with most teachers since they somehow associate it with weakness. An indulgent teacher, however, is not one who is so permissive as to be inactive or emasculated but one who, on the contrary, is strong enough to soften a cutting (and therefore ineffective) reply, to diminish punishment in order better to correct, and to bear with students who are weak-willed but still struggling.

This "gentleness of the strong," moreover, promotes a serenity that every "gentleman" possesses. The old saying goes: A bad man is easy on himself and hard on others; a good man is hard on himself and hard on others; and a saint is hard on himself and easy on others. Every gentleman, of course, is not a saint, but every saint is a gentleman. And, in a sense, the teacher should aim at the virile gentleness of the saints, the gentleness that sweetens effective reproof.

Not only does the kind teacher correct the erring, but he also compliments the student who does good. Realizing the difficulties of doing well, he is easily pleased, quick to see virtue where it exists in however tenuous a way, apt to smile and give the handclasp and word of congratulation, rather than to sneer at and criticize efforts that are only partial successes. St. Paul says not only "Weep with those that weep" but also "Rejoice with those who rejoice" (Rom. 12:15).

Cheerful words in class can set the tone for fruitful, not frivolous, work, since they are spoken from a loving and helpful heart. In fact, it is a two-way process: kindness (trying to see what is good in students) can as often lead to a loving heart as a loving heart can lead to kindness—it becomes a kind of benevolent circle, expanding with each act of will and heart.

Pascal says that "the heart has reasons which the reason cannot understand," describing a wisdom that is from the heart rather than the head, from loving rather than studying. It is a wisdom consonant with kindness.

The kindness of the good teacher should be available to all, just as "the Lord's mercy reaches all flesh, reproving, admonishing, teaching, as a shepherd guides his flock" (Ecclus. 18:12 [Sir. 18:13]). Common experience would indicate that those who most need a word of encouragement are those who are least likely to get it. It is easy to be kind to the good or the suave student, the one who has a happy, responsive personality or who is gracious or appreciative. But it is the slow student, the one who fails consistently, who becomes surly and suspicious, who *"knows* that nobody likes him" — he is the one to whom it is difficult, naturally speaking, to be kind and understanding. The more forsaken, the more desolate he is, the more should the teacher "leave the ninety-nine" to seek him out and help him to overcome his anxieties, worries, and fears.

The saints have had the selflessness to do so. Of their kindness Shakespeare could have been speaking when he said:

> The quality of mercy is not strained,
> It droppeth as the gentle rain from heaven
> Upon the place beneath.[3]

Sometimes the student, with a false bravado assumed to hide the shame of his weakness or need, drives the unsuspecting teacher to an unkindness that reassures the "outlaw" and vindicates his cynical belief that he is right, that he should not have expected anything but persecution from anyone. And perhaps he is lost for good.

Cautions on Kindness

Although teachers are guilty of giving too little, rather than too much, praise, the line between kindness and weakness is at times indeed fine. Flattery, for example, is unwholesome praise, given

---

[3]   William Shakespeare, *The Merchant of Venice*, act 4, scene 1.

without sincerity or where it is really not merited. The teacher's motive may actually be selfish—a desire for easy popularity or some type of repayment. Pope in his *Moral Essays* says satirically:

> Not always actions show the man: we find
> Who does a kindness is not therefore kind.

He could have expanded by saying: he who has only the *appearance* of kindness in his flatteries is actually *unkind*, for he ruins a student with overconfidence, based on an exaggerated assessment of his capabilities or accomplishments. He is simply *using* his students, not serving them.

The same could be said of a teacher who, moved by antipathy, fails to give credit where credit is due or who, swayed by emotional attachment rather than solid merit, hoards his praise for the precious few.

Beside the danger of selfishness, which can lead to abuses of unkindness or doting, the teacher must control the passion of anger, for it has been responsible for more sins against kindness than any of the other passions.

Finally, there is the problem of insensitivity, plain obtuseness that fails to see the opportunities in which to exercise this virtue. Perhaps prayer, a will to develop the habit of kindness, and a closer study of the students will, with time, overcome these obstacles.

Eventually he may understand the meaning of Wordsworth's words in *Lines Composed a Few Miles above Tintern Abbey* and, with him, look back at

> That best portion of a good man's life,
> His little, nameless, unremembered acts
> Of kindness and of love.

8

Firmness

Firm in All Things and Assured

Two men look at a delftware bowl. One says it is convex in design; the other says it is concave. That it can be both at the same time is no great difficulty, unless a lapse in logic leads one to conclude that any one characteristic of a thing excludes all others.

The critics of Christianity seem to have made this rather elementary error, denying to Christians the virtues of strength and firmness because they also believe in charity, humility, and kindness.

Nietzsche proposed, for example, that Christianity weakens a man and paralyzes his energies, that the whole system of Christian morality is a plot of the resentfully weak to undermine the powerful with such "unmanly" virtues as docility: teach the strong to be considerate, and you can conquer them, so to speak.

Karl Marx's evaluation was no more profound. To him, religion appeared to be the "opium of the people," an enervating narcotic that debases and softens man.

Neither man realized that the Christian, without becoming schizophrenic, believes in both kindness and firmness, and that the two virtues are inseparable because both are facets of the spiritually courageous man. He is out for a greater conquest than either Nietzsche or Marx could envision; he aims at the conquest of the

Kingdom of Heaven, a Heaven-storming project that depends not on his own strength but on a supernaturally invigorated power from God.

It is not surprising, then, that the Christian teacher who, when viewed from one angle, is gentle, kind, and forgiving is also firm and steadfast when the occasion requires it.

This firmness, an aspect of the virtue of fortitude, is necessary if a teacher is to establish discipline, and discipline is a necessary condition for learning.

Knowledge is communicated when progress is orderly—step two follows step one. Skip a step, and the ranks become ragged and confused; soon they are scattered in four different directions. Every marching group, for its own good, needs a drummer to keep it in line. And the teacher through his firm leadership is the guide in the classroom.

Students themselves realize the necessity for order and organization; and they know that, left to themselves, they will not maintain it. They want a teacher who will not be pushed around: with St. Paul, the good they will to do, they do not; and the evil that they do not will, they do. Their natural reaction is to kick against the goad, but they know that the goad is for their good: "A colt untamed turns out stubborn; a son left to himself grows unruly," says Ecclesiasticus ([Sir.] 30:8).

If the teacher is firm, he will command the students' respect. Without this respect, the teacher is doomed either for an early nervous breakdown or the ruination of his classes.

"Exhort, and rebuke with all authority," say the Scriptures. "Let no one despise thee" (Titus 2:15). This authority will be based upon a certain dignity; on maintaining a sound teacher-pupil relationship; on force of character, straightforward and manly; on devotedness to the students, the teacher's best and perhaps subtlest means to attain student cooperation; and virtue, that all-embracing character to which students will unconsciously respond.

Effective Means of Establishing Order

A "virtuous teacher" does not simply fall into an ordered classroom; he must take means to attain order.

He must set up specific regulations for class procedure and then stick to them. They should be carefully considered, important, and limited in number.

If there are too many, the students in the class will be unable to keep all of them, and, from disregarding a few, they will soon be disregarding them all; the teacher will find himself involved in so much red-tape punishing violations, he will soon grow panicky, lose control of the class, and be changed to a new school the next year, if not sooner.

Once a few important rules, however, are laid down, the teacher must check violations. If they are not important enough to enforce, they are not worth making in the first place.

Among the most necessary regulations should be a certain amount of silence. Instruction comes through hearing. If the din is so great that the students cannot hear, there will be very little teaching taking place.

It is the kind of problem that can grow worse: the racket can be ominously increased over a short period of time, until the students have developed the habit of talking out loud in class without permission or of chatting cozily in a back row of the classroom.

Demanding obedience to the class routine will stem most of the other abuses, the demand being made not for its own sake but in the interest of good order. Once the teacher is recognized as master, teaching can go on easily. Rapport between teacher and class will *follow*, not precede, such mastery.

Challenging work with meaningful assignments will lead to the students' intellectual development. A feeling of progress, a feeling that they are actually "learning something" and not simply running through mechanical forms, will develop curiosity and interest, which are the best means of attaining discipline and order.

Diligence, "a high estimation or love" of learning, will do more than anything else to aid the teacher to do his job. "Tend the flock of God, which is among you," says St. Peter, "governing not under constraint, but willingly, according to God" (1 Pet. 5:2)—good advice for both teacher and pupil.

A student who is *with* the teacher will help to enforce good order. And if both teacher and student are interested in ideas, they will soon be trotting voluntarily in the same direction.

A firm teacher knows the weaknesses and strengths of his students and, while being just, adapts to their needs with charity and common sense, with a view to their welfare—otherwise he is a tyrant, not a teacher.

Punishments

Establishing order is not enough; it must also be maintained. To do so is a problem that again raises the question of punishing students. "Folly is close to the heart of a child, but the rod of discipline will drive it far from him," says Proverbs (22:15). But discipline needs regulating.

Punishments should be appropriate, given with a view to correction, not to revenge. The easy "Write out such and such a thousand times" is not only unconsidered; it is useless and rash in most cases. Sanctions should be thought out beforehand; otherwise, they are usually too numerous or involve too much or are too severe.

Their purpose should not be to "break" students, most of whom have a high sense of honor that leads them to see that their conduct earns a reprimand at times. Their innate feeling for justice may make them appear stoic during a punishment, but in reality, they may be accepting without a murmur what they know they deserve.

On the other hand, the teacher must be certain that he has the guilty party (*the* guilty party, by the way, not a *whole class*—unless he wants to antagonize all of them) and that the discipline is deserved. Otherwise, he risks doing an injustice from which his authority will never recover.

When punishments are necessary, they should be given with at least a modicum of decorum: calmly, coolly, and with dignity of manner, not with the rampaging spite of a bully picking on the defenseless.

Aspects of Firmness

Firmness in a teacher will be normally clustered with other qualities, among which regularity or constancy ranks high.

Firmness implies uniformity of action: application to all and at all times. If a teacher is consistent in his classes, he can develop habits of order in pupils, since habits come through repetition, not only in the pupils but in the teacher himself.

Punctual, organized, he will avoid the upsets that go with fluctuating standards and capricious conduct. A certain equanimity, that is, a balance of soul, will come to his aid when the unexpected does crop up.

Soon after their first contact with him, students will inevitably provide the teacher with a test of some kind to see if they can ruffle him; if they can, they will be boss. Being prepared for any kind of calculated or scatterbrained chicanery, and meeting the situation calmly, will give the teacher an ascendancy that will go far in keeping future order.

A sense of humor will also help him in a crisis. If, for example, he is able to view a situation objectively and see in it its essentially humorous aspect when there is one, he will not waste misdirected anger on it. And it will be passed off, perhaps unnoticed; he will save himself from blowing up nonessential foibles of students into catastrophic proportions.

Little things are sometimes important, though, and the good teacher practices vigilance, keeping his eyes open for anything *sub rosa* that might be detrimental to a particular student or to the class in general. He need not spy or develop anxieties, but he should not be so much in the clouds or so naive that he fails to see the obvious.

His best means of order, however, is his own interest in learning, reading, studying, organizing. After all, he is not a policeman; he is in the classroom because he is so filled with the importance and the value of ideas that he wants to share them, to communicate them to the student.

Where teaching is going on, discipline pretty much takes care of itself, the students are persuaded to love the truth, and distractions are anticipated and removed.

The Weak Teacher

A teacher may be weak either through lack of firmness or through a mistaken idea as to what firmness is.

An embarrassed, unsure, or perplexed air on the part of a teacher is bound to communicate itself to the students (and they will usually take advantage of such a teacher; unfortunately, students are not by nature very kindly individuals toward the weak in either their own ranks or in the ranks of their teachers).

Thoroughness of preparation will, to a great extent, help him to overcome such an attitude; but if it does not, the students will get the upper hand—a state resulting in the utter rout, through panic or discouragement, of the young teacher.

Students, for some reason or another, are prone to boasting about how many teachers they have sent to the hospital or driven out of class. Granted, they are inclined to exaggerate; yet the teacher who condescends to them through weakness is in an unenviable position, to say the least.

The opposite attitude, undue severity, can be just as disastrous. A human being is constitutionally unprepared to maintain an attitude of severity for very long. It is too hard on the nerves. Soon it degenerates into anger, violence, obstinacy, an alienated class, and either stomach ulcers or the abandonment of teaching.

If a teacher is inhuman or cannot control himself, he can hardly hope to control other human beings for very long. And students, despite, at times, suspicions to the contrary, are eminently human and require the same loving care that the teacher exercises in his other human relationships.

One variety of severity may be grounded in fright, a defense mechanism based on the principle of the survival of the fittest; whereas another may be based on misguided vanity (usually the teacher who prides himself on discipline as though it were an end in itself is guilty of this type) or on sheer opinionatedness, a Napoleonic complex uninhibited by self-knowledge, true learning, or an informed mind. Of this type, Shakespeare says: "Man, proud man, drest in a little brief authority . . . plays such fantastic tricks before high Heaven as makes the angels weep."[4]

But whatever its basis, the severity of a teacher cannot withstand the erosion of student resentment for very long.

---

[4]   William Shakespeare, *Measure for Measure*, act 2, scene 2.

Loving Firmness

Love, united with firmness, is the answer to the correct conducting of any classroom. "You are the substitutes of the parents," says St. La Salle. "God has established you the spiritual fathers of the students you instruct; then have for them the firmness of a father and the gentleness of a mother" (Meditation for the Third Sunday after Pentecost).

Kindness, the other side of the coin, must radiate from the same teacher who is just, constant, and firm, so that he can exercise the apostolate recommended by St. Paul: "Reprove the irregular, comfort the fainthearted, support the weak, be patient towards all men" (1 Thess. 5:14).

9

Humility

With Humility Have Self-Esteem

We was to be umble to this person, and umble to that; and to pull off our caps here, and to make bows there; and always to know our place, and abase ourselves before our betters. And we had such a lot of betters! Father got the monitor-medal by being umble. So did I. Father got made a sexton by being umble. He had the character, among the gentlefolks, of being such a well-behaved man, that they were determined to bring him in. "Be umble, Uriah," says father to me, "and you'll get on. It was what was always being dinned into you and me at school; it's what goes down best. Be umble," says father, "and you'll do!" And really it ain't done bad!

Thus did Charles Dickens's infamous and oily Uriah Heep, in *David Copperfield*, embody the writhing servility and damning caricature that is sometimes mistaken for the virtue of humility.

Poor Uriah really "done bad," however, whether he realized it or not, and, after a lifetime of "umbleness," not surprisingly, knew nothing of humility.

Humility is a virtue that is peculiarly Christian and, consequently, has had a history of misunderstanding and disfavor. Homer's Achilles, pouting in his tent because he has been dishonored and ready to see his own Greek army demolished so that he and his friend Patroclus could have the honor of singlehandedly wiping out the enemy Trojans, could really have as little use for true humility as Uriah.

Even the great pagan philosopher Aristotle, in his portrait of the "magnanimous man" of the *Nicomachean Ethics*, presents a hero blemished by pride.

But neither pagan "Christian" nor pagan Greek is equipped to define humility fully, that virtue by which a man, in imitation of Christ's practice of the revolutionary new concept of humility, judges and acts in accordance with a correct opinion of himself. The catch is in the word *correct*; for neither Uriah nor Achilles could see himself clearly or really do justice to himself.

Humility is truth: the truth about oneself and a proper estimation of oneself in the light of this truth. Such an estimation is possible only if one sees himself as God sees him, in both his greatness and his weakness — the greatness teaching thanks to God, who gave it; the weakness teaching dependence on God, who can make up for it.

In a sense, humility is an interior virtue, existing in the proper intellectual conception of oneself but at the same time unselfconsciously revealing itself externally in acts that manifest subjection as a creature to God.

Uriah's cap-holding and bowing were the conscious imitations of spontaneous, inner-directed acts of the truly humble man; the one, sprung from selfishness, based on an exaggerated opinion of self; the other, from selflessness, based on a just estimate of self.

If the will deliberately chooses "self-effacement," it is because it sees that man has in himself no real cause for self-aggrandizement; on the other hand, Ecclesiasticus says, "With humility have self-esteem; prize yourself as you deserve" (10:27 [Sir. 10:28]).

Man's dignity, then, rests on the fact that while he is the epitome of visible creation, he is also the image of God. His humility is a matter of gratitude, simple and objective, for gifts both natural and supernatural that God has given him. "It is God," says St. Paul, "who of his good pleasure works in you both the will and the performance" (Phil. 2:13).

The good teacher, therefore, realizes that his capabilities and virtues come from God and that without Him he can do nothing. "What hast thou that thou hast not received?" St. Paul could well have been addressing the successful teacher. "And if thou hast received it, why dost thou boast as if thou hadst not received it?" (1 Cor. 4:7).

Humility will aid the teacher to combat pride, which will, in turn, tend to undo his work as an effective educator and cause great harm to the students. Aware that in the classroom he is not by himself, he takes to heart the wise evaluation of good work: "Neither he that plants is anything, nor he that waters, but God who gives the growth" (1 Cor. 3:7).

Effects of Proper Self-Evaluation

A proper self-evaluation should lead to a teacher's feeling both humble and confident; and these virtues should, in turn, overflow into action (unlike Uriah's) that is effective in good teaching. For example, he should become a little more lenient in judging students. "We are all frail," says the *Imitation*, "but see thou think no one more frail than thyself" (I:2:4).

A common quirk of teachers is to harangue students for failings that they themselves are guilty of: the talky teacher lowers the boom on the talky pupil; the teacher who himself fails to prepare classes takes no excuses for homework not done; the teacher who slips into the room a second after the bell has rung has no sympathy or willing ear for latecomers.

Since students are young and still in the process of building habits, they should certainly have more excuse than the teacher.

If the teacher sees the student as a creature of God, he will also give him the courtesy that his dignity as such deserves. And if he places himself in his rightful place before God, he will induce order into his relationships, and, as a consequence, he will be easy to live with and to like.

A teacher who respects his students will naturally exhibit goodwill, trying to understand them in order to help them because they are important.

Even when they do not rise to hopeful expectations, the teacher will understand that the good in them is there and must be pursued with perseverance until it is activated.

It is not easy to keep industriously giving out energy and sympathy when some kind of return is not made; but real faith and confidence in the innate worth of a human soul, even when a student does a good job of hiding it, will lead the teacher on to greater resolution and with at least the hope of doing some good, even if it is unknown or develops much later in the student's life.

Finally, he should be loyal to students, respecting their confidences and putting good faith in their never-ending but honest promises (perhaps everlastingly being broken) to do better in the future.

Humility will affect not only his attitude toward the student but his attitude toward himself. The humble teacher will not become overly elated by success in the classroom (a probable prelude to ensuing troubles) or depressed by failures. If his students do not walk away with the prizes, or if he maintains discipline on only a precarious basis, or if he fails to be popular with either students or fellow teachers—all after his best efforts—he will accept his limited success as well as his limited failures.

Above all, humility will lead him not to take himself overseriously. Robert Burns says in his poem "To a Louse":

> O wad some power the giftie gie us,
> To see oursels as ithers see us!
> It wad frae monie a blunder set us
> And foolish notion.

Which simply means we would see ourselves objectively and, consequently, with humility.

Lack of Humility

From the standpoint of sheer practicality, humility is an essential virtue for any teacher, young or old, expert or novice, brilliant or slow, because the only alternative to it is pride, the root of all evil and of most of what goes wrong in a classroom.

Pride in a teacher may be expressed in one of two ways: in either underestimating or overestimating one's natural or spiritual excellence. The rarer form is of the Uriah Heep brand, which, either through sloth or hypocrisy, delights in self-depreciation. Such a teacher refuses to put to work his God-given talents for the school or the students. Unreasonable fear of failure may be at the root of it. But after a teacher has made his representations to the administration, pointing out his qualifications or lack of them, he should cooperate in the teaching or extracurricular assignments he gets, doing the best he can with them and leaving the rest to God—and the principal.

Some principals are easily browbeaten, and a teacher may sometimes get out of jobs that he is the best (if not perfectly) qualified for on the faculty—perhaps for some subject, for the school paper or yearbook, or for athletics or for one of the dozens of other activities around a school that must be taken care of by somebody. He does a real disservice to the good running of the school when he refuses to exercise the ability he has, disregards it, or hypocritically pretends that he has less talent than he has—for example, not developing his personality or not using his mind in study and teaching. Coleridge, in his poem "The Devil's Thoughts," says that the devil's "darling sin is pride that apes humility."

Of course, doing too much, for the wrong reasons, can be as bad. Fawning and trying to find favor is a form of calculation or groveling that is beneath the teacher's proper dignity.

Honest, selfless, wholehearted cooperation is a form of humility. The teacher who "takes his five periods a day" and calls it quits has not fulfilled his obligations. Official functions (with the dull duties that go with them), graduation ceremonies (with all the dressing up), plays, concerts, athletic contests, meetings of faculty or extracurricular groups, drives (those unavoidable and distasteful—but necessary—money collections), and a thousand other details and snippets of red tape that swallow up one's time—all require at least a measured cooperation, or a school could not continue.

However, sins through excessive reticence are not nearly so common as those committed through vanity, based on a rather unruly notion of one's excellence. Despite the warning that "God resists the proud, but gives grace to the humble" (James 4:6), the proud teacher can puff himself up, out of all proportion, in his own mind.

He is the real problem: his students are neither bright enough to benefit by his intellectual brilliance nor slow enough (a rarer case) for him to show his talents by "bringing them along"; the school or the city or the courses are not congenial to his peculiar genius; the students or the faculty or the principal does not appreciate him—in a word, he is a thorn in everyone's side and demonstrates the truth of the *Imitation*: "It is better to have little knowledge with humility and a weak understanding, than greater treasures of learning with self-conceit" (III:7:3).

With such delusions of grandeur, it is impossible for such a latter-day solipsist, who holds himself beyond warning or correction, to accept from anyone else any kind of advice that could help.

"Oftentimes it is very profitable for keeping us in greater humility that others know and reproach our faults," says the *Imitation* (II:2:1). But if, in the midst of classroom chaos, a teacher insists that he has order or that the fault is in the students, nothing more can be said.

Such a one usually rests complacently on nonexistent virtues, talents, and powers, looking down tolerantly, but blindly, on faculty and students, until the students, who are ultrarealists, drive him out of class. Even then, he may hold someone else responsible for the fiasco, venting his jealousy of other teachers in backbiting or disparagement of their successes. He will blame everyone but himself.

If a proud teacher *is* talented, he may also pervert his actual success by foolish ambitions, looking for continual thanks from students or principal, recognition, distinctions of one kind or another, priority of treatment, unreasonable advancement; whereas the humble teacher is satisfied in the good done, the talent used, not letting his left hand know what his right hand does.

In any case, the proud teacher will eventually sabotage his own efforts; when he fails, he will wilt, becoming sad or angry or discouraged.

A rarer form of pride, but a catastrophic one in a teacher, is spiritual—the sin of the Pharisees. It may be particularly common with the young, new teacher who belongs to a religious congregation and has just come fresh from the novitiate or scholasticate.

Forgetful of the advice "Esteem not thyself better than others, lest, perhaps, thou be accounted worse in the sight of God, who knows what is in man" (*Imitation* I:7:3), such a teacher becomes indignant with evidences of real or imagined evil or weakness in students or fellow faculty members.

He may be unduly shocked or may damage a soul through harshness where understanding is necessary. The probability is that such a teacher may do just as much harm by eventually developing a cynical attitude toward the student as he did by his prudishness.

For a teacher to appear inordinately surprised by evidences of human weakness is to suggest implicitly that the seed of sin was somehow inadvertently omitted from his soul when he came into the world. A little honest soul-searching should set him right.

Humility, like many other virtues, walks the razor edge, tending to slip into pride of one kind or another; so that it becomes impossible for a teacher to practice it unless he keeps one eye always on Him who said, "Learn of me, for I am meek and humble of heart" (Matt. 11:29) and the other on himself, with prayer as the steadying influence and the echo of the *Imitation* in his ears: "Trust not in thine own knowledge, nor in the cunning of any man living, but rather in the grace of God, who helps the humble and humbles those who presume on themselves" (I:7:1).

10

Patience

Do You Also Be Patient

Sick, discouraged, and ridden by a specter of defeat, Milton, in the sonnet "On His Blindness," consoled himself with the thought that "they also serve who only stand and wait."

If an unconvinced sound of shuffling feet seems to provide a soft obbligato to his words, most teachers would be ready to forgive him his solecism, since they know that there is nothing quite so exasperating as waiting out difficulties or letting good take its own time in getting done.

Yet every teacher also knows that he must, like Milton and in spite of his natural desire to "get on with it," learn to mark time patiently, while God's work in the classroom goes on quietly, effectively, without fanfare, and, on occasion, in apparent failure.

Only patience will maintain in a teacher that interior calm and peace of soul necessary for this facing of afflictions and disappointments of one kind or another, so that, paradoxically, real progress in class can be made in God's good time and in His way.

For a teacher to face problems patiently is really the hallmark of his maturity, for to possess one's soul in humble self-discipline is the result of a developmental process, the work of a lifetime.

Usually, the youthful enthusiast devises grandiloquent schemes to satisfy all contingencies and to achieve in one fell swoop all the ends of education. And it sometimes takes a while for him to settle down (after a period of recovering from the wounds suffered in noble experiments) to the controlled effort that yields results.

Everyone wants to accomplish something, and it is "only natural" that a little misguided zeal will settle for nothing less than success "right now!"

But there's the rub: the Christian teacher must think supernaturally; he cannot act "only naturally." A kind of animal good nature can be fundamentally beneficial if one is to acquire patience; but there must be much more — not just an easy disposition or a refusal to lose one's temper, but a positive and virile virtue; not just a personality with a low threshold for contentment, but one with a grace-given control of self.

Like humility, the virtue of patience is, in essence, an effect of hope, for it trusts in God to come to its aid; it awaits His help with confidence.

It has nothing to do with a sterile stoicism that will not become irritated simply because it is bad for the nerves or because it is cynically convinced that no good will come of getting disturbed by anything; rather, as St. Paul says, Christians "exult in tribulations, knowing that tribulation works out endurance, and endurance, tried virtue, and tried virtue, hope" (Rom. 5:3-4).

Patience, then, endures difficulty not only with hope and love but also with joy — not neurotic joy but joy such as St. James commends: "Esteem it all joy, my brethren, when you fall into various trials, knowing that the trying of your faith begets patience" (1:2-3).

Patience towers up in the spirit, not in the temperament. The stolid, phlegmatic teacher can lay no claim to the virtue of patience because he lacks the vitamins or the imagination to get excited about things; nor is the energetic, animated person, quick and responsive in situations, necessarily impatient. Outlook is all.

Patience is neither determined by temperament, nor is it dependent on circumstances. A teacher who is never crossed by providence, pupils, or principals (perhaps because a cutting tongue, natural ability, or a pleasant personality protects him) may not merit the label *patient*.

On the other hand, the one who, because of some culpable mismanagement or blunder, has justly had his whole world come tumbling down has as little reason to boast of his great patience in affliction. St. Peter says: "What is the glory if, when you sin and are buffeted, you endure it? But if, when you do right and suffer, you take it patiently, this is acceptable with God" (1 Pet. 2:20).

Ultimately, patience, like humility, generosity, and kindness, is selfless. The patient man can afford to remain calm, since he is doing God's work, not his own. He does not need a flourish of trumpets, since he has no need for personal recognition. No palpable success need provide him with steppingstones to the fulfillment of some personal ambition, a gratified ego, or a better-paying job.

Since he has no private interests that can be threatened, he does not anxiously imagine envious hostility where it does not exist.

He can "bear fruit in patience" (Luke 8:15), remembering the words of St. James: "The farmer waits for the precious fruit of the earth, being patient until it receives the early and the late rains. Do you also be patient" (5:7–8). He can steadfastly put up with the present in patient expectation of future blessings.

Patience in the Classroom

A teacher with patience is well on the way to leading students in what is good, since he does not expect perfection from imperfect strivers. They are allowed some leeway, with time to get where they are going.

In their slow progress as weak human beings, students are prone to taking one step backward for every two steps forward; but eventually, with a teacher's coaxing and confidence, they seem, amazingly enough, to get to the goal he wants them to reach.

This patience with their stumbling efforts is based on the teacher's sense of his own imperfections and weaknesses; as a consequence, he can be sympathetic with their struggles. St. La Salle pointed out the necessity of such communal understanding when he said: "The weakness of a man is great, but that of the youngster is much greater, because he has less rational control and because human nature is more lively in him, more inclined to enjoyment of pleasures of sense" (Meditation for the Third Sunday after Pentecost).

Time is needed to teach irresponsible boys to be trustworthy, the shiftless to be dependable, the scatterbrained to concentrate his powers, the foolish to act with good sense.

To demand rashly that a poor student learn at the same rate as the good one is as unrealistic as expecting the sinner to become a saint overnight. It has happened at times, but the event is called a miracle. Miracles in the classroom are rare (at least, as far as we know), being accomplished with painstaking patience and energetic labor.

Once the teacher has resigned himself to making haste slowly, he will himself learn careful kindness, reasonable correction, thanks for small gains.

He will welcome students' questions and difficulties, since these are the obstacles to their advancement.

He respects their point of view, approves it when it is right, considerately refutes it when it is wrong, corrects it when it is uninformed—all of which takes patience and calm.

Patience will dictate a teacher's attitude not only toward students but also toward his very methodology. Distrustful of so-called crash programs, which unwisely hope to accomplish wonders of learning without proper consideration for either the nature of the student or the appropriateness of the matter, he remains methodical in procedure so that what is learned is learned well.

He sticks to fundamentals so that the basis for future work is firmly laid. He gives his students the essentials so that the groundwork is secure.

The eccentric and the peripheral aspects of a subject are sometimes enticing (and, in fact, at times useful for stimulating interest), but they can be as useless as going on to advanced work before taking the necessary preliminary steps.

Since solid teaching is frequently the outcome of careful planning, the patient teacher prepares his classes thoroughly, consistently, and with perseverance. Patience is needed to correct and grade papers, to grind out the necessary part of preparation, but this aspect of teaching is crucial to success.

Perhaps patience is most necessary when, after a teacher has followed good advice, recommended methods, and the dictates of charity, students remain impervious either to ideas or the love of virtue. Wooden and insensible, they may not respond to the most persevering efforts.

A teacher's simple inability or sickness may result in failure too.

But in either case, he murmurs, "*C'est la vie,*" picks up the pieces, and keeps trying.

It may be that great graces and vigorous growth are taking place interiorly, without visible results. In any case, most real successes in teaching may be the hidden ones. At least, that is a consoling thought, one that, like patience, lessens disappointment, while encouraging the teacher and spurring him on to continued efforts.

A word should also be said about the necessity for a teacher to have patience with the other members of the faculty and with individuals in administration. Theoretically, he belongs to a "community of scholars" blessed with the advantages of education, maturity, and experience.

Unfortunately, like the students in the class, the members of a faculty have virtually the same friction points. The only difference is that the teacher has the benefit of authority in class but has no such advantage with his peers: each will have his own method of teaching (each of the methods recommended with equal infallibility), each will have his own solution to problems, each will be generously endowed with irritating foibles and eccentricities—all of which means that they are human beings, muddling along in more or less haphazard fashion like all the others.

On the other hand, each will have his strengths and virtues, his insights, and at least a measured desire to share them. With patient sifting of these various qualities, a teacher may learn how he can best contribute to, as well as draw upon, the pooled resources of the faculty.

Impatience

"If thou dost not make use of the buckler of patience on all sides thou wilt not be long without a wound," says the *Imitation* (III:35:1). The warning could not have been given with more appropriateness to anyone than to the teacher, for once he loses calm, he loses his class. The chaos in himself tends to spread to the students.

Like a charioteer whose horses break into a disordered gallop when he loses his head and gives the horses theirs, the teacher is responsible for his own ruin. "You cannot better instruct your students than by giving them good example," says St. La Salle, "and repressing within yourself every movement of impatience" (Meditation for August 13).

Impatience leads the teacher to the wrong treatment of students on every side: he makes mistakes and will not admit them; he acts rashly, frequently in anger, and without having the facts to make a valid assessment of a situation; he balks at the slightest disagreement; he becomes annoyed on the slightest grounds; he judges in haste and repents at leisure, only to compound his error in judgment by tolerating, in reparation, abuses that should never be tolerated; he antagonizes students with dictatorial, censorious, but ill-advised, decrees. In short, impatience is a shorthand formula in how to achieve in a class situation the greatest misery for the greatest number.

Not the least unhappy will be the teacher himself. Impatience only intensifies his troubles in class. With his failure, brought on through his own imprudence (that vainly tries to hide weakness with blustering bombast), the embittered teacher distills black melancholy that simply feeds his weakness. He resorts to the easy excuse, "My patience is exhausted," when in reality, his problem is that he did not have any patience in the first place.

His only solution is manfully to undertake the practice of self-control, being "patient in tribulation, persevering in prayer" (Rom. 12:12), and assiduously following the program set down in Ecclesiasticus:

> Be sincere of heart and steadfast, undisturbed in time of adversity.... Accept whatever befalls you, in crushing misfortune be patient; for in fire gold is tested, and worthy men in the crucible of humiliation. Trust God and he will help you; make straight your ways and hope in him. ([Sir.] 2:2–6)

11

Seriousness

Be Simple and Serious

The habit may not make a monk, but it helps to remind him of who he is and how he should act if he is to be in harmony with everything that the religious robe symbolizes.

Likewise, the externals of dress and manner do not make the teacher, but they do frequently reflect his attitude toward his profession; and it is by them that, right or wrong, his students, their parents, and his fellow faculty members are going to judge him.

He cannot very well expect people to believe him if, while protesting that he considers himself to be engaged in a work of profound significance and tremendous consequence, at the same time he behaves pretty much like an irresponsible clown.

Kings, statesmen — in short, anyone who deals with weighty matters — are expected to take such matters seriously, and it is not unreasonable to expect, in turn, that this seriousness will be externalized in some way. "One can tell a man by his appearance," says Ecclesiasticus; "a wise man is known as such when first met. A man's attire, his hearty laughter and his gait, proclaim him for what he is" (19:26-27 [Sir. 19:29-30]).

It is true that stressing form for form's sake is hypocrisy. But, as St. La Salle shrewdly observed to the crude young men he was trying to shape into teachers, "Exterior gravity indicates interior wisdom befitting persons of the teaching profession" (Rules, chap. 23). He knew that the impress of ideas on action is inevitable, that the public instinctively knows this, and that no teacher can therefore safely ignore the dictates of decorum.

The teacher contracts for a momentous responsibility: the formation of human beings through education. Unmolded, sometimes even spiritually or intellectually misshapen, these adolescents, rife with myriad passions and talents, passively await sorting out and development by some perceptive or forceful guide.

They are souls redeemed by the blood of Christ; souls who are the hope of the Church, of society, of their families; souls over whom the teacher can exercise a decisive influence. There can be no room for bunglers; souls are at stake. No wonder, then, that the good teacher should be characterized by seriousness, since his is a serious job.

"After the sacred priesthood," says St. La Salle, "the vocation of the Christian teacher is among the most excellent in the Church and is the most capable of sustaining it" (Meditation for August 13). He is continuing in the work of Christ Himself, who spent the years of His public life teaching.

If, then, he is to cultivate, strengthen, and polish the expectant, pliable raw material of the classroom, the teacher cannot afford to take his task lightly, wantonly manipulating or tampering with souls as though he were engaged in some innocuous game.

Forming the adult in the child after the image of Christ is the teacher's unparalleled métier and prerogative, two conditions that rule out of the teaching ranks the incorrigible butterfly or the refuge-seeking incompetent. It illumines in the teacher an ever-present, perhaps subliminal, but interior, warning: "Teacher at work at all times."

The characteristic of seriousness in a teacher is therefore a product of his own conviction as to the importance of his function in society; and it regulates and governs all of his exterior conduct: his speech, his actions, his appearance—that result that occurs when a person is permeated with the fire of an ideal.

Characteristics of the Serious Teacher

Seriousness must not be identified with sadness or the "countenance like a jail door": it is cordial in the deepest sense, arising from heartfelt interest in the progress or failure of students in intellectual as well as spiritual pursuits. Through interest, the serious teacher proposes well-considered solutions to student problems, offering them with the sincere desire to help.

But no student will rely upon a teacher who lacks evidence of sound judgment. After all, the youngsters are going to school because they are learning. They do not have the experience or the ability at their stage of development to evaluate situations and find proper answers by themselves.

If they sense in a teacher the same emotional immaturity that exists in themselves, they are not likely to depend on hearing any particularly satisfying counsel from him. "If your demeanor be simple and serious," says St. La Salle, "they will be convinced that your interior is well regulated and that you are competent to educate in a Christian spirit" (Meditation for Retreat). Seriousness will give proper weight to a teacher's words.

Even in disposition, the serious teachers are consistent in character. Always the same, unafflicted by strange vagaries, whimsical moods, or crotchety ways, they are readily approached by students who know what to expect from them.

If one day a teacher is sympathetic, another day sarcastic, and on a third day totally indifferent, the student will stop trying to figure out whether this is a "good day" or a "bad day" to approach him and will keep his own counsel, perhaps in a matter that requires a mature opinion. A teacher must be worthy of confidence and trust.

Maintaining order in a classroom also requires seriousness. In a complex mental syllogism, the students will frequently (and rightly) conclude that a teacher who can control himself—possesses his soul in peace, so to speak—can control the class.

In the fencing for dominance between teacher and students that inevitably preludes the actual teaching that may eventually be done, the new teacher who means business and gets down to it immediately has won at least the first encounter.

This seriousness of purpose must continue and become a habit. Students wait out the first few weeks of class quietly evaluating and judging a teacher. When he has merely donned a temporary mask of seriousness in order to establish discipline and then, confident that he is in control, lapses into levity, he may lose once and for all the authority that he thought he had so easily gained. The measure of wisdom in the old pedagogic saw "Don't smile before Christmastime" vindicates the importance of seriousness.

Pursuing a course constantly and calmly, with deliberate order and not haphazardly by fits and starts, the teacher will accomplish wonders of teaching with a class. Classes that learn, that are taught, will feel the thrill of accomplishment and will respect not only the teacher's work but the teacher himself.

The effort required to teach in this manner demands that the teacher first imbue himself with the importance of his work and then take serious means to do it. If he has little respect for his profession, not considering it worth the bother of careful preparation or so inconsequential that the classroom becomes an amusement hall, he has only himself to blame when students vie for the spotlight and the laughs.

He has lost a sense of proportion: once this calamity has occurred, he has prepared the way for the apotheosis of poor teaching—ridiculous in serious matters, he becomes serious in ridiculous matters.

Trouble Spots

Gilbert and Sullivan satirically proposed that "things are seldom what they seem; skim milk masquerades as cream." But one does not have to be a connoisseur to see through such a masquerade; there would be even less sense in cream posing as skim milk.

Likewise, a teacher, through a kind of perverted humility, should not denigrate himself or his profession by paying no attention to appearances just because appearances sometimes deceive. "Let your light shine before men," said Christ, "that they may see your good works and give glory to your Father in heaven" (Matt. 5:16).

Appearances are important, if only in an oblique way. Even such a trait as a teacher's manner of walking has significance. Children skip, run, and jump, reflecting their inner impetuosity and naturally high spirits; but a teacher walks with poise, reflecting calm.

Children, when seated, sprawl or squirm or slither, cross their legs, uncross their legs, sit with them doubled beneath them, wriggle over the arms and backs of their chairs—in short, evidence youthful restlessness; but a teacher who is guilty of such posturing becomes ridiculous. He should be able to control his movements, avoiding scarecrowlike, as well as effeminate, gesticulations.

Standing on top of desks, chairs, even windowsills and radiators, some teachers have been known to adopt Napoleonic attitudes that certainly command a splendid view of a classroom and demand universal attention from startled students; but a buffoon also attracts attention—usually catcalls. Such indignity can only bring deserved obloquy down on such a clownish teacher.

The opposite fault is as bad: the stiffness of a marble statue, the reflection of fear or such deep abstraction that the students are soon either roused to raucous enjoyment of the mental "absence" of the teacher or lulled to sleep.

With eyes modestly cast down on his teaching notes, the teacher withdraws to his own private isolation booth, leaving the students unwatched. This kind of overdecorousness is rare, but it crops up occasionally. Seriousness requires interested vigilance, not the obdurate insensitivity of a deaf, dumb, and blind attitude.

Relationships with students outside of class are more apt to demand caution than they do in class. Even when a teacher may join in their activities in order to draw out students (and they *do* reveal themselves most plainly on the playing field or in extracurriculars), he must always remember that he is not on their level.

He is not a boy again. He is always the mature, self-contained guide. To lose control of himself in anger, impatience, or giddiness is to undermine that respect that he must preserve on the ball field if he is to maintain his authority later on in the classroom when the games are over.

Good sense would dictate that taking part in student competition should be very rare, if it occurs at all, and that the teacher be proficient in the activity.

The adolescent's innate tendency to hero worship can be exploited; but, on the other hand, it may boomerang: a teacher who is respected in class may lose his ascendancy over the students outside of it. If he has so little respect for himself that he is willing to reveal his weakness, even of a physical nature, before students, they will soon take him at his own valuation.

Familiarity breeds a contempt that no teacher may risk. He must always be on the qui vive, forestalling by reserve any lessening of student esteem.

Such errors in judgment usually result from a teacher's misguided effort to be "liked" as a person, as an individual, for himself; but he can never be really "just a person"; he is always the teacher, just as a father or mother is never "just a person" to his or her children. Teachers always have a unique character by the very relationship. This is their special glory—being what they should be.

It would be as foolish for the teacher to try to give up the teacher-pupil relationship in which his "grace of office" inheres as it would be for parents to sacrifice the parent-child relationship in order to be "pals" with their children. A teacher may even reach the point where, to his own destruction, he can fool himself into feeling that he is "one of the boys"; but the boys will never really be taken in by his equivocal role.

A serious teacher must be serious even in his dress: if he must "act his age," he must also "dress his age." Gaudy colors and a dashing cut to clothes are characteristic of the youngster who is hovering on the edge of maturity, but who is still, in a sense, on the playground.

But the teacher is launched on his career, his work has started. The very term "a business suit" conjures up a certain savoir faire, an adult dignity. The teacher who "means business" in class should dress the part. If he wants to "look like a kid again," he more than likely wants *to be* a child again. But the profession of teaching is closed to children.

No one goes to an important interview, a responsible job, or a public appearance of some consequence without careful attention to personal cleanliness, neatness, and appropriateness of dress. Every day, the teacher is engaged in such an interview, job, and appearance—in his class—and if he ignores the dictates of common decorum, he would risk rejection by his students.

Seriousness, then, extends to everything from cut of coat to tone of voice, from classroom activities to extracurriculars; but, above all, it springs from an attitude of mind.

Teaching requires a serious attitude, a steadfast maturity, a certain finesse won through wisdom that commands respect, inspires confidence, stirs up diligence, and enables the teacher to "speak and exhort, and rebuke, with all authority" (Titus 2:15).

12

Silence

A Time to Be Silent, a Time to Speak

Shape nothing, lips; be lovely-dumb:
It is the shut, the curfew sent
From there where all surrenders come
Which only makes you eloquent.

So wrote Gerard Manley Hopkins in his poem "Habit of Perfection." In this quatrain, he suggested both the nature and the purpose of true silence; it is the novitiate of speech, charging man with both wisdom and a responsibility to communicate it effectively.

Like the yang and the ying, those inverted and contrasting complementary commas of the Chinese that unite to make a single circle, silence and speech are inseparable.

Empty silence is merely preparation for the booming of the empty barrel, which traditionally makes the loudest noise; but active, thoughtful, prayerful silence that fulfills itself in speech is the proper return to God for this great gift.

For it is a great gift, that which distinguishes man from beast. Aesop, Montaigne, and Swift to the contrary, the lion and the tiger will continue to snarl, the dog to bark, and the bird to twitter endlessly and without meaning. But man has been so created as to be able to label the sounds he utters and to use them to communicate to others what he finds in the secrecy of his soul to be noblest, most beautiful, and most significant.

Words have conquered continents, challenged tyranny, expressed love, revealed God's truth, bestowed knowledge and understanding on the ignorant. How true is the encomium voiced in Proverbs: "Like golden apples in silver settings are words spoken at the proper time" (25:11).

But the catch to speech, as to silence, is in the qualifying word *proper*. "There is an appointed time for everything, and a time for every affair under the heavens," says Ecclesiastes; "a time to be silent and a time to speak" (3:1, 7).

Silence consists not so much in keeping mum at all times as in saying the right things at the right time—and, conversely, proper speech consists in keeping silent when one should. St. La Salle, in a letter to a young Brother, said: "It is great knowledge to know how to keep silence at the right time; there will be no order in your class, unless you observe silence in it."

For a teacher, who must use words to communicate ideas, the virtue of silence will be exercised in circumspect speech, a speaking in the "right way" so that an atmosphere for study can develop interested application on the part of the students.

Speech in the Classroom

The faculty of saying the right thing in class is the fruit of right thinking—operating, of course, on the facts stored up through concentrated study.

A teacher will win respect for knowledge only if he respects it himself; and a teacher who has so little respect for it that he refuses to take time to discover truth himself has no place in a classroom. "The mouth of those who speak falsely shall be stopped," say the

Psalms (62 [63]:12) — but sometimes not before a good deal of harm has been done.

The teacher, in the silence of his study, must make himself responsible for the subjects he teaches.

He must also have the ability to impart his knowledge. Personality will play a part in the procedure, of course; but a teacher can have success without becoming a one-man entertainment committee. It is more important that he speak concisely, with a precision and brevity that will communicate ideas to students clearly, than that he amuse them.

St. Paul asks, "Unless with the tongue you utter intelligible speech — how shall it be known what is said?" (1 Cor. 14:9). A good question.

The answer, obviously, is that it cannot be known. Students are already enveloped in their separate little clouds of unknowing when they enter the classroom, without having their confusion compounded by a teacher who is intellectually fogbound or who delights in the cryptic question or the windy explanation.

It is impossible to be too direct or too logical. Students, still struggling for ordered thinking, come with a built-in blender that will readily enough scramble ideas presented to them.

If a teacher works with them slowly, clearly, step by step, he will have a good chance of getting an idea across to them.

Brevity, which is the "soul of wit," is also the key to methodical teaching that results in the students' learning.

When he has explained a subject as well and as economically as he can, the teacher must prod the students' minds with well-considered and leading questions. He must become a kind of *Socrates-cum-veritate*, foreseeing the usual difficulties and pointing questions to them, so that, with solutions, the way is cleared for understanding.

A Christian teacher *does* believe in truth and in the ability of the mind to attain it; he believes in absolutes and, consequently, unlike the relativists, in answers.

Not that such answers are always complete or simple. In fact, for a teacher to evade difficulties or to invoke his dogmatic authority is a form of intellectual dishonesty that may backfire when the student later realizes the problems but no longer has the proper guide to help him solve them. He may at such a point repudiate everything—the truth as well as the falsehood—that he identifies with such a teacher. St. La Salle warns the teacher to "give the means of persevering after they shall have been taken from under your watchful eye" (Meditation for the Third Sunday after Pentecost).

Great prudence is required in this matter: young students, impatient of fine distinctions, are anxious for absolute answers; they reject the qualifications. And the teacher's tendency is to give them what they want.

On the other hand, to suggest problems that are neither opportune nor appropriate to the age or to the development of the students is to create doubts and uneasinesses with which they are not as yet able to cope.

Questions and directed discussions, therefore, need careful preparation; otherwise, the answers may be haphazard, confusing, or wrong.

Silence, while checking pointless garrulity, does not eliminate discussions with students in class, or questions on the part of the student, but it does require consideration—a consideration that is leisured enough to result in accuracy. "Do you see a man hasty in his words?" says Proverbs. "More can be hoped for from a fool" (29:20).

Strong words, but true, and reinforced by Ecclesiastes: "Be not hasty in your utterance.... Let your words be few" (5:1).

The good teacher also sticks to his subject. Examples taken from baseball games or current movies or politics may be useful to invigorate a dying discussion; but when they become entertaining ends in themselves or means of whiling away the time till the bell for the end of class rings, they defeat their purpose.

Unless applicable to the point at hand, miscellaneous information, no matter how erudite or impressive, should be suppressed. "Flaunt not your wisdom at the wrong time," says Ecclesiasticus ([Sir.] 32:4), since it is not enough to say the right thing, it must also be said at the right time.

Delivery is important too. The teacher may not be the "strong, silent type," but that is no excuse for exposing students to a barrage of strident, wordy discourses that fray the nerves of listeners, annoy, and ultimately repulse them.

A mellifluent voice is difficult enough to listen to if it swells on and on; wisdom dictates that even with a pleasing voice, good diction, and training in public speaking, a teacher is shrewd to cut down on his talking, especially if he has a tendency to become carried away with his own rhetoric.

The teacher who is silent will have a silent class: the longer and the louder he talks, the higher will the decibels become, until the teacher is barely holding his own against the reverberating noise of the classroom. Through loud, excessive talking, he also wastes his energy, reduces his effectiveness, and ends the day hoarse of voice and physically exhausted.

"It is easier to be altogether silent than not to exceed in words," says the *Imitation* (I:20:2). But in lieu of absolute silence, which is impossible in our modern school system, at least restraint should be exercised.

There are certain times when it is a teacher's duty to speak—either in correction or in commendation. Such occasions should be handled quietly and quickly. He should also require and encourage attention and concentration with a word here and a word there.

A teacher working quietly at a blackboard, for instance, back turned to the class, not only violates the vigilance demanded by prudence but also invites general, albeit silent, disorder behind him while he is obliviously going his own way.

When class regulations are flagrantly violated in one way or another, a reprimand is in order, silence notwithstanding.

In general, if speech remains moderate, becoming, calm, even though energetic, and exercised for the good of the student, it cannot be said to violate the dictum "Silence is golden."

Effects of Silence

Perhaps the chief effect of a teacher's silence in the classroom will be to win him the respect of the students. They will be ready to listen; whereas if he keeps up an incessant babble, any remarks of significance he has to make tend to become drowned in the sea of drivel.

Once the students are conditioned to the fact that when the teacher opens his mouth to speak, he will say something worthwhile, they will gradually become habitually receptive and develop an attentive attitude.

From this initial accomplishment, the teacher can hope for a tractable class that will heed any recommendations that he makes and will actually profit by them. Not only will they follow his advice, but they will follow his example, looking to him for the right word, the clarifying idea, the perceptive insight.

With such a classroom milieu, intellectual development, the purpose of the school after all, can more easily be achieved. And the teacher will find that the crutches of discipline—shouting and ranting—are not needed; order will reign, daydreaming will be limited, and he will feel that the scholastic millennium has arrived.

Teachers who keep their mouths closed also learn how to listen ("swift to hear, slow to speak"), a function of every teacher who has done student guidance work. The student's self-therapy, "getting things off his chest," is possible only if a teacher makes himself accessible and listens with considerateness.

The silence that is his shield in the classroom becomes his buckler outside of it.

Talkative Teachers

"He who guards his mouth protects his life; to open one's lips brings downfall," says Proverbs (13:3)—a fitting epitaph to the teaching career of many chatty, prattling, disorganized new teachers. Such a teacher takes the risk of irresponsibility or imprudence every time he speaks. It is a risk that he cannot afford to take.

Why?

Whether or not he realizes it, the teacher is Sir Oracle to his class, and his words go well beyond the classroom. The students pass them around among themselves and retail them at home to their parents. Eventually, a teacher may hear them quoted in public to his own surprise, pleasure, or perhaps, embarrassment.

Many times, the original remark has undergone such a strange sea change that it is virtually unrecognizable. If this is true about some harmless remark, imagine what happens to the ignorant or indefensible one.

Teachers are not the only ones who have heard the quotation "Out of the abundance of the heart the mouth speaks" (Matt. 12:34), and they should not feel abused if they are judged by what they sometimes foolishly say.

Particularly shocking to students and the public is any teacher who in his speech resorts to crudity or coarseness. No gentleman, let alone a teacher, should be guilty of such behavior. "A man who has the habit of abusive language," says Ecclesiasticus, "will never mature in character as long as he lives" ([Sir.] 23:15). Simple good sense, based on good taste, would dictate that such a person is a danger in the classroom.

The same could be said of the cold, the cutting, the dictatorial, the boring, or the ridiculous—none of them can really do effective work; whether their weakness is the result of pride, presumption, or misplaced self-sufficiency, they are ripe for a sad awakening amid the shards of class discipline.

Not only the *what* and the *how* of a teacher's speech is of importance but also the *where* and the *when*. Talking to fellow faculty members is fine; it keeps up friendly relations—but not outside in the corridor during or between classes, when he should be earning the tuition that the parents pay for education.

The corridor conferences during school hours are just as out of order when they are held with individual students under the guise of child guidance. Christ left the ninety-nine for the one lost lamb; but His ninety-nine were "the just."

The law of averages would indicate that the teacher's whole class needs his attention at all times; and, in this case, leaving the thirty-five or more in the classroom—even if they are supposed to be saying the Rosary by themselves or doing some type of busy-work—for the one is a brash failure in prudence and justice.

Some other time should be arranged for individual attention if it is needed and if it comes within the province of the teacher's duties.

This holds true of interviews with parents: school hours are the students', not the parents'. Appointments with them should be rare, brief, and, above all, when necessary, scheduled at a convenient time.

Silence grips primarily the reins of speech; but it should equally hedge in the desk thumper, the door slammer, the heel pounder—the generic noisemaker who can unnerve whole corridors of classes and all of the students in them.

Quiet. Reserve. Dignity. These are essential characteristics of the good teacher. And he should frequently repeat to himself the judicious injunction of Ecclesiasticus! "Young man, speak only when necessary, when they have asked you more than once; be brief, but say much in those words, be like the wise man, taciturn" ([Sir.] 32:7-8). If he does this, he will never have to fear those words of Christ that ring so ominously in every teacher's ears: "Of every idle word men speak, they shall give account on the day of judgment" (Matt. 12:36).

About the Author

Br. Luke M. Grande, F.S.C. (1922–2006), was born in Minneapolis and was a member of the Brothers of the Christian Schools. He received his bachelor's degree in English from Saint Mary's College in Winona, Minnesota, in 1944, his master's degree in English from Loyola University in Chicago in 1948, and his doctorate in philosophy from Saint Louis University in 1956. He had a distinguished career as an English, religion, and Latin teacher at De La Salle Institute in Chicago; Central Catholic High School in Vincennes, Indiana; Christian Brothers College in Saint Louis; and Christian Brothers College in Memphis. He was president of Christian Brothers College from 1964 to 1970. He later taught at colleges in Florida. He was a prolific author and also wrote and published books of poetry.

Sophia Institute

Sophia Institute is a nonprofit institution that seeks to nurture the spiritual, moral, and cultural life of souls and to spread the gospel of Christ in conformity with the authentic teachings of the Roman Catholic Church.

Sophia Institute Press fulfills this mission by offering translations, reprints, and new publications that afford readers a rich source of the enduring wisdom of mankind.

Sophia Institute also operates the popular online resource CatholicExchange.com. *Catholic Exchange* provides world news from a Catholic perspective as well as daily devotionals and articles that will help readers to grow in holiness and live a life consistent with the teachings of the Church.

In 2013, Sophia Institute launched Sophia Institute for Teachers to renew and rebuild Catholic culture through service to Catholic education. With the goal of nurturing the spiritual, moral, and cultural life of souls, and an abiding respect for the role and work of teachers, we strive to provide materials and programs that are at once enlightening to the mind and ennobling to the heart; faithful and complete, as well as useful and practical.

Sophia Institute gratefully recognizes the Solidarity Association for preserving and encouraging the growth of our apostolate over the course of many years. Without their generous and timely support, this book would not be in your hands.

www.SophiaInstitute.com
www.CatholicExchange.com
www.SophiaInstituteforTeachers.org

Sophia Institute Press® is a registered trademark of Sophia Institute. Sophia Institute is a tax-exempt institution as defined by the Internal Revenue Code, Section 501(c)(3). Tax ID 22-2548708.